2 ½ℓεσ
Hoph

o Cirencester

BRAYDON FOREST

o Malmesbury

Liddington
? Mons
Badonis

Dyrham   Barbury

Chippenham

R. AVON

W. Wansdyke   E. Wansdyke

Bradford-
on-Avon

MENDIPS   Wodnesbeorg

R. Axe   Camerton

o Buckland
Dinham

o Amesbury

Glastonbury o   Penselwood   Old Sarum

Winchester

R. Parrett

Fosse Way   o Sherborne   Totton

Fosse

Road

Dorchester

andun

THE SAXON CONQUEST
OF
SOMERSET AND DEVON

THE SAXON CONQUEST

OF

SOMERSET AND DEVON

by

H. M. PORTER, M.A.

JAMES BRODIE LIMITED

Brodie House, Queen Square

Bath, Somerset, England

First published in 1967
© *H. M. Porter*

Made and Printed in Great Britain by
COWARD & GERRISH LTD., LARKHALL, BATH, SOMERSET

Preface

THIS small book attempts to set out all that is known, which is little, and most of what has been said, which is much, on a particularly obscure part of the history of the West Country. The subject has again aroused controversy in the last few years because of the very interesting contributions of Professor H. P. R. Finberg and Professor W. G. Hoskins, as well as the work on Wansdyke by Sir Cyril and Lady Fox, with the counter-arguments of Dr. J. N. L. Myres. Much, too, is likely to be heard in the next year or two of the startling theories of Miss Vera I. Evison in her book, *The Fifth-Century Invasions South of the Thames*, published in 1965. Such views as I have reached are tentative and as temporary as all historical conclusions turn out to be.

A certain amount of repetition has been unavoidable. Early writers, from Freeman onwards, have been referred to and quoted where their views are valuable; where no new evidence has been produced to contradict their conclusions, they are fully entitled to a hearing. On such matters as the events of 658 and 682 and the occupation of the Quantocks early views still seem to me to be valid.

I wish to thank Mrs D. E. D. Beales for dealing with some knotty pieces of Mediaeval Latin.

H. M. PORTER.

Bath.
27th July, 1966.

Contents

CHAPTER ONE

Ceawlin

577. *In this year Cuthwine and Ceawlin fought against the Britons and killed three kings, Conmail, Condidan and Farinmail, at a place which is called Dyrham; and they captured three of their cities, Gloucester, Cirencester and Bath.*[1]

IN these terse words, and no more, does the *Anglo-Saxon Chronicle* record the great West Saxon victory over the Britons, the most important of the three battles which were the turning-points in the early history of England. As the *Chronicle*, in its several versions, was started in Alfred's reign about A.D. 890, over three centuries later, the lack of detail is understandable.[2] Among the earthen fortifications we can see to-day on the shoulder of the Cotswolds, six miles north of Bath and beside the so-called Jurassic Way, the West Saxons met with overwhelming success in their great drive into the heart of the Celtic West. The prosperous, wealthy land, once full of Roman villas, now Gloucestershire, was theirs, and, most important of all, they had reached the Severn and permanently divided the Britons. It was up the Severn Valley that they next advanced. With Gloucester, Cirencester and Bath in their hands, it was easy for the West Saxons to acquire the part of modern Gloucestershire east of the Severn: this area was lost later, probably in 628, and became part of the Mercian sub-kingdom of Hwiccia.[3] It is a startling fact, however, and one needing explanation later, that it was not for at least another century that they reached the River Tone and built Taunton, only 40 miles from Bath.

To the Britons, the result of the battle of Dyrham or Deorham was the loss of their last chance of unity. Geographically, the Welsh of Wales were separated for ever, by Saxon territory and the sea, from their kinsmen in West Wales, that is, in most of Somerset, all Devon and all Cornwall. They were not separated culturally or ecclesiastically, and other links, even political ones, such as a shadowy titular leadership, may have remained for a short time,[4] but any political and military cohesion for common action was a thing of the past. Dyfnaint or Dumnonia was bound to look after itself without help, protected for the present by marshes and forests. The petty kings in the West and South-West, of whom Gildas had complained so savagely about 540, had failed, and never again would they all have a chance to combine against their heathen common enemy.

Sixty or seventy years before this, things had gone very differently. At Mount Badon,[5] wherever that was, about the year 500 or the year 517, the Britons had hurled back the Saxons of the Upper Thames Valley (who had come to the Abingdon region, some along the Chilterns and some probably up the Thames), and they had done this in so completely crushing a way that many Saxons had gone back to Germany.[6] The Celts had shown that, united and well led, they could overthrow the invader utterly. Unfortunately for them, "the inter-tribal warfare characteristic of the Celtic temperament", as G. M. Trevelyan describes it, which had revived with the tribalism that followed the waning of Roman influence, was in abeyance only temporarily.[7] (In this respect, the Saxons after the conquest were as bad as the Celts, but they apparently knew, what the Celts did not, when inter-tribal warfare was something that they could afford.) Gildas may have been right, too, when he said that a moral rot had set in. He has always been looked upon as a man with the outlook and temperament of an Old Testament prophet born out of time, but he very acutely remarks that the unexpected recovery at Mount Badon and "the remembrance of such a terrible desolation" as had preceded it had "caused people in public positions to live orderly. When these died out, this generation, ignorant of the past, ignored truth and justice."[8] He had seen these things happen with his own eyes. It was very much a late post-Badon generation that lost at Dyrham.

This result, however, may have been inevitable. Though the Saxons as a race had taken about half-a-century to recover from the blow at Mount Badon, in that period the tribe or tribes that had landed from their five ships at Totton on Southampton Water about 495 under Cerdic and Cynric had taken Old Sarum in 552 and had proceeded to cross and to possess themselves of Salisbury Plain. They had then won a victory over the Britons in 556 at Barbury "Castle" on the Ridgeway five miles NNW of Marlborough (and in sight of Liddington Castle four miles away, the reputed scene of Mount Badon) and so had achieved permanent contact and perhaps unity, if an uneasy one, with the Saxons of the Upper Thames.[9] There had been other campaigns before 577 in other directions, for instance, in Bedfordshire, Buckinghamshire and Oxfordshire.[10] Thus it seems likely that the Britons at Dyrham had to fight Saxon forces that had far greater resources in man-power to call upon than their grandfathers had had to face at Mount Badon in 500 or 517—allowing for the families that had gone back to Germany. Whatever the cause, now, after Dyrham, the great question had been settled for ever: England, though not all Britain, would be Teutonic, not Celtic, English, not Welsh.

It is not clear how far south of the Bristol Avon, if at all, Saxon control reached after 577, or whether the area "controlled" was colonised or merely became tributary. We shall probably have to form quite new ideas as to the old face of Somerset, of the nature of a Saxon conquest and of the nature of a Saxon frontier, if we are to get anywhere near the truth. Many historians have placed the boundary on the River Axe, but the Axe originates at Wookey Hole, two miles west of Wells, only half-way between the old boundary of Selwood Forest on the east and the sea on the west. Some have said that the Saxons, like the Romans, must have wanted the Mendips for the sake of their lead mines, but the lead mines at this time are believed to have been deserted.[11] Evidence of Saxon occupation of North Somerset at this period is practically non-existent, with two possible exceptions. It seems likely, but not absolutely certain, that the Saxon cemetery above Camerton, beside the Fosse Way, dates from long after 577. Mr. W. J. Wedlake, who excavated the site, wrote, "The cemetery, judging from the orientation of the graves and the cross on two of the bracteates found, was probably a Christian one and is the largest cemetery of its type to be thoroughly excavated in S.W. Britain".[12] It was a civilian cemetery of 109 graves, apparently in use in the sixth and seventh centuries A.D. If it was Christian, it must have been later than 634, when Birinus started evangelising the West Saxons. A single grave at Buckland Dinham is said to have been a pagan interment of the sixth century.[13] Mr. L. V. Grinsell says that these burials were somewhat in the pagan tradition, but mentions elsewhere that pagan methods of burial continued well into the Christian period. In his view these burials must have been started after 658.[14]

They are south of the Wansdyke: pagan or not, they need not prevent us from thinking that at one time, perhaps for a short period, the Western Wansdyke from Portbury to Bath was the boundary between Saxon and Briton, a mark on the ground rather than a defensive work, although it certainly links three camps.[15] Offa's Dyke comes to mind as a comparable frontier, intended in its day to be as impassable as the Iron Curtain, the chief sanction being terror of mutilation rather than armed force. The Eastern Wansdyke, starting eastwards on Morgan's Hill outside Devizes, is separate, and its remains, having been cut from the chalk, are far more formidable as an obstacle than the trifling remains west of Bath: the two Wansdykes probably belong to different periods.[16] Of course, a great feature of the seventh century was the preoccupation of Wessex with its northern frontier. Both Wansdykes face north.

A different theory with regard to the date and purpose of the Western Wansdyke has been put forward by Sir Cyril and Lady Fox.[17] In their view it was not created by the Britons against the Saxons after 577, but by the West Saxons against the Mercians after 628. Under that date the *Anglo-Saxon Chronicle* records that "In this year Cynegils and Cwichelm fought against Penda at Cirencester and afterwards came to terms". (Sir Frank Stenton says that Penda was not yet a king, but possibly a noble fighting for his own hand.) This seems to be the only incident which could be the point at which the West Saxons gave up all claims to control Gloucestershire east of the Severn, and that area became part of Hwiccia, a sub-kingdom of Mercia, ruled from Worcester. (The area was practically coterminous with the mediaeval diocese of Worcester.)[18] It is possible that the West Saxons had to agree to keep south of a line, marked by the Wansdyke, leaving the Avon Valley below Bathford to the Mercians. This would have been an advantage, if the Avon was in use for navigation, as it seems to have been from Roman times, to the now Mercian towns of Bath and Bristol. Otherwise both sides would have been better off with the Avon as a frontier and with only fords to guard. Penda would not have made the Saxons build a bank to keep him out.

If the Fox theory is right,[19] soon after 577 the West Saxons must have had land, some of it later lost, between the Avon and the southern edge of the Mendips, with access to it mainly through Bath and down the Fosse Way: it would have been between 300 and 400 square miles. We believe the Fox theory to be wrong—Penda could not have imposed a boundary like the Wansdyke in country he had never seen—but what the Saxons gained permanently from the battle of Dyrham, apart from the great advantage of having divided the Britons for ever—a Saxon rather than a West Saxon benefit—is not obvious. That they lost Bath and south Gloucestershire to Hwiccia and so to Mercia, either in 628 or soon afterwards, is certain. They had not claimed all North Wiltshire, as we shall see. If the Britons did build the Western Wansdyke against the West Saxons, they cannot have contemplated manning it continuously throughout its length or for long at all:

the resources of an empire are required for that sort of thing. Probably there would have been time and opportunity for Saxon farmers to infiltrate into North Somerset, at least between Wansdyke and the Avon, between 577 and 628, supposing that the area was in fact sealed off by Penda and his Mercian free-booters in that year, with the Avon as a boundary, but there is no evidence of this infiltration worth anything.[20] The archaeological finds seem to show that the Saxons in the year following 577 settled in the southern Cotswolds only and not in North Somerset.[21] After 628 they had no bridgehead into Somerset at Bath: they would have had to enter the present county through Selwood, which was crossed by at least two prehistoric trackways still in use and one Roman road.[22] One does seriously doubt whether the battle of Dyrham had much to do with the Conquest of Somerset, except in so far as it brought the West Saxons into the Bath neighbourhood for 50 years and made it inevitable that sooner or later they would enter Somerset in force from one direction or another.

It seems clear that Ceawlin can have had no firm grip on the basin of the lower Avon, except possibly between 577 and 591; whether the battle of Fethanleag in 584 was a defeat or not, he was expending considerable energy, it seems likely, either in Cheshire or in Oxfordshire. On the other hand, if this battle was at Fretherne, 8 miles south-west of Gloucester, the fact that it took place at all would go to show how insecure was Ceawlin's grip on South Gloucestershire itself. Then in 591 some of his people, led by Ceol, who was made king of part of Ceawlin's territory, revolted against him. This is thought to have been a manifestation of tension between the Salisbury Plain West Saxons and the Upper Thames West Saxons.[23] In 592 at Wodnesbeorg (almost certainly Red Shore, where the Ridgeway crosses the Wansdyke, thought to be the scene of one of Ine's battles, too) Ceawlin was driven out, and the next year he, Cwichelm and Crida were killed.[24] (Cwichelm's memorial is the name Scut-chamer Knob or Cuckhamsley on the Ridgeway S.E. of Wantage.) With all these misfortunes building up around him, it is unlikely that Ceawlin had more than a slight and temporary control, if that, over either side of the Avon.

To sum up, the probability seems to be that the Wansdyke was dug as the best boundary the Britons thought they could get for themselves after 577, and that the Avon was the Mercian boundary after 628. There seems to be no evidence that parties of Saxons drifted into north-east Somerset at this period. The settlers using the cemetery at Camerton must have come down the Fosse Way or up the Fosse Way at some time, but archaeology cannot prove that this happened before the last half of the seventh century. The scarcity of archaeological sites is astonishing and significant.

How the Britons, or West Welsh, were organised and governed in the south-western peninsula south of Dyrham and the three "Chesters" of 577 cannot be known. Lady Fox says that the Roman cantonal organisation probably survived into the fifth century,[25] but local kingships arose that must have had some sort of relationship with the tribal areas on which the cantons were based. About 540 Gildas found a number of local kings to denounce. Undoubtedly the chief and perhaps the only settled government in the south-west was the Kingdom of Dumnonia, including Devon, Cornwall and a part of Somerset. It lasted as a kingdom, though with diminished territory, until 710 and as a Celtic kingdom or kingdoms, probably feudatory, in Cornwall until the tenth century. Mr. A. L. F. Rivet says that characteristic pottery indicates that Dumnonia once stretched as far as the Glastonbury marshes and had a common frontier with the Dobunni[26] who occupied the present Gloucestershire and parts of neighbouring counties. This common frontier must have been the Somerset River Axe: Ptolemy in the second century A.D. referred to this river as in the canton of the Dumnonii.[27]

No doubt the Durotriges of Dorset, who were not finally defeated until 614[28] (or later, if the chronology of the A.S.C. is wrong), had some sort of organisation still, and this must have covered a part of Somerset, for Ilchester, famous for the large number of Roman villas near it, had in the third century been made the second cantonal capital of the Durotriges, additionally to Dorchester. As for north Somerset, it is impossible to say what the situation was after Roman government collapsed. The Romans had at one point artificially created the canton of the Belgae, with Winchester as its capital and Bath as its other chief city. It stretched across Wiltshire and included north Somerset and south Gloucestershire, taken from the administrative control of the Dobunni. Something so artificial must surely have collapsed early. [29]

As to Glastonbury, there was a document which William of Malmesbury saw there, purporting to be a grant of land to Glastonbury in 601 by a King of Dumnonia. This document is referred to later in another connection. The probability is that it was antedated by three-quarters of a century, or even an exact century. [30] However, even if it was genuine and correctly dated, it would not, as some have thought, prove that Glastonbury was in Dumnonian territory. Geraint, an historic King of Dumnonia, about 705 granted land to Sherborne when it was definitely in Wessex. [31] But it is likely enough that Glastonbury was in Dumnonia in 601, with the great swamp of Brent Marsh between it and the Axe at the foot of the Mendips, and that the great Celtic shrine, physically insignificant but already with its mysterious odour of sanctity, was regarded by the Dumnonians as under their special protection. In any case, it mattered little what were the tribal origins of the West Welsh, whether they were Dobunni, Durotriges or Dumnonians: they were all in the same boat now, but the next disaster was long delayed.

The south-western peninsula was still one of the lands of the Britons, of the Wealas or foreigners, as the Saxons called them, of the Cymri or comrades, as they called themselves. Devon was very thinly peopled and the whole area was somewhat drained of strength by emigration to Brittany. The ancestors of these people had arrived long before the Roman occupation, in the late third and the second century B.C. from north-western France. [32] They, or at least the lower classes, had gone on using their own Celtic tongue from which modern Welsh is, and the Cornish language was, descended. Their chief city was Exeter,

Isca Dumnoniorum, the former cantonal capital, but now somewhat decayed,[33] like so much in Britain. In fact, the Britons
had lost their "Romanity" and were rapidly reverting to type as
tribal Celts. As R. G. Collingwood says, "their material and
spiritual possessions were ... deeply and increasingly tinged
with Celticism".[34] "So far as the meagre evidence goes," says
Lady Fox, "their mode of life differed little from that of the Iron
Age," and she adds that the Dark Ages were full of petty local
kings and independent dynasties, ill-organised, so that Dumnonia,
when at last seriously attacked, could not offer strong resistance
to the West Saxons.[35] Trevelyan sums it up: "Geography
inverted the course of history, making the Celt barbarian and the
Saxon civilised."[36]

Far more important than his language (which has never been
the medium of any really great work of literature or learning,
whatever the Welsh Nationalists may think), the Celt kept his
religion and in a singularly pure and spiritual form. When Rome
ceased to govern Britain, she ceased also to regulate the religion
of the Romano-Britons, and the fervent religion of South Wales
(and of Ireland, which the Romans had never touched) was very
little institutionalised: it was based mainly on the small monastery
or minster of a dozen or so ascetics, with no standardised Rule.

A dozen little huts would cluster round a primitive chapel, as at
Glastonbury or Tintagel, and the inhabitants would minister to
the religious needs of the district. Christianity in Roman Britain
had been mainly urban and, although there may have been small
groups of Christians in Somerset at Bath and Ilchester, rural
Somerset does not seem to have been evangelised until the fifth
and sixth centuries. It was in those centuries, the Age of the
Saints, that missionaries from Wales (especially Llantwit Major),
Ireland and Brittany made their impact on the South-West. As
the West Welsh often named churches after the local "saint" or
cleric who first came to a district as a missionary, there are traces
still of St. Congar at Badgworth near Axbridge and at Congres-
bury, of St. Bridget at Brean and Chelvey, St. Dubricius or
Dyfrig of the Arthurian legends at Porlock, of St. Decuman at

Watchet, St. Petroc at Timberscombe and St. Beuno at Culbone. In Street is an area called Leigh, which was, according to A. G. C. Turner, originally Lantocai, after St. Cai. He mentions that the parish church of Street was formerly dedicated to St. Gildas.[37] In contrast, "in Cornwall alone," says Lady Fox, "174 out of 212 ancient parishes are dedicated to a western saint and about 50 in Devon."[38] As Dr. Ralegh Radford has said, "Somerset takes its place in the Celtic world which became Christian in the sub-Roman age and such evidence as we possess falls into the common pattern of the age".[39] Christianity also became a part of Celtic nationalism: no Briton would teach the hated Saxon the Christian faith. Why save these barbarians from the Hell they so richly deserved? Rome had to do the missionary work herself. Luckily, between 577 and 658 when the Saxons really entered Somerset in force, Birinus and his followers converted them.[40]

The Delay

Why did the West Saxons not make any further military or political advance for 75 years after the battle of Dyrham? Some of them must have been inhabiting at least the southern Cotswolds down to Bath for a matter of fifty years (577 to 628) under the West Saxon sovereigns. One reason must have been that they were fairly well occupied with struggles against other Saxon kingdoms, especially Mercia. In addition, to a people with, probably, as much land as they could cultivate, in Hampshire, Wiltshire, Berkshire and parts of Oxfordshire and Dorset, Somerset cannot have been particularly attractive, especially as there would have been the large, though not populous, West Welsh kingdom of Dumnonia to cope with. As it turned out, the south-westward expansion was a long job: started in 652, it did not really end until the battle of Hingston Down in Cornwall in 838, or, formally, until Athelstan fixed the Tamar as the West Welsh boundary in 926. At the same time he cleared the Welsh out of Exeter.

The uninviting nature of seventh century Somerset must now be considered. From the southern edge of the Mendips there stretched miles of marshland, dotted with islands, with the

Polden Hills as a long, thin peninsula in the middle. The marshland, which was, and is still, easily flooded in winter,[41] ran inland
as far as Langport and Taunton. There were vast areas of woodland and of scrub. The wooded part of the mediaeval Forest of
Selwood does not seem to have been very wide,[42] perhaps four
or five miles on the average, but it stretched from Malmesbury to
Wincanton. Besides the trackways and the Roman road already
mentioned, the enigmatic road, probably never completed in its
middle lengths, but planned from Bath to Poole Harbour, must
also have passed through it in the Longleat area. All these
existed in the seventh century. The Fosse Way ran parallel with
the western edge of the Forest throughout its length, but at some
distance from it. In fact, Selwood was more a social and cultural
than a military barrier,[43] but clearing woodlands would have had
to precede cultivation, and much of it is woodland still.

The first edition of the Ordnance Survey map of Britain in the
Dark Ages, published in 1935 (but not the second edition in 1966),
based on geological certainty and ecological probability, shows
areas that, because of the nature of the soil, may have been covered
with trees and scrub in Saxon times.[44] In addition to Selwood,
there is shown a rough square of woodland with Glastonbury in
the north-west corner and sides about 12 miles long, running
north, south, east and west: there is also a considerable extension
from the south-west corner right down to the Blackdown Hills.
(Sherborne, the new diocese to which Ine appointed Aldhelm as
bishop in 705, was "be westan Selwuda", but east of this equally
great area of woodland.) There was a five-mile belt of fairly clear
country west of the dense belt of Selwood and Braydon Forests,
which ran from Cirencester right down into the present Dorset.
The enormous marshes or "moors" from the Mendips almost to
Langport and Taunton have already been mentioned: that to the
north of the Poldens used to be known as Brent Marsh and that
to the south of them is still called Sedgemoor. Further west, the
moorlands of the Quantocks and Exmoor (if the West Saxons
had only known) offered poor farming prospects. The Saxons
were farmers first and foremost, and Somerset to them must have

presented a daunting prospect of back-breaking toil, of years and years of marsh-draining and forest-clearing, before a satisfactory return could be gained.

We must consider, too, the probability that racial frontiers and military-political frontiers were not the same; quite probably there was seldom any recognisably real "frontier" at all and the Saxons infiltrated among the West Welsh as blobs or cells, each producing in time another colony or cell moving a few miles further south-west before clearing land for a new family farm or village. Some of Ine's laws provide for this sort of thing. R. H. Hodgkin says that progress against the West Welsh was "as much an agricultural as a military operation—felling of woods, building of towns and reclaiming of heavy lands in river valleys".[45] A little later he adds that the expansion of Wessex was the result of gradual settlements rather than of scientific campaigns. "The Saxons seem to have spread west much as did the Americans and Canadians in the nineteenth century." They occupied the lands they wanted, often those which they first cleared in the river valleys. The Britons on the higher lands were mostly content to let the newcomers alone.[46] Oman refers to Ine's laws as showing that many of the West Welsh were clearly being left undisturbed as landowners, small and great, and he mentions that "Some became royal officials and served in the King's comitatus, though they retained a separate name and status".[47] The adoption of Christianity and the sheer length of time the conquest had been going on had ended the days of extermination and complete expropriation, if there had ever been such days.[48]

To sum up the first stage of the conquest, it seems that there is no evidence available to prove that Ceawlin's victory at Dyrham in 577 gave him the land between the Bath Avon and the Somerset Axe: Freeman, and others, must have accepted this idea because they felt bound to find a new frontier somewhere.[49] With our present knowledge we must believe that Dyrham gave the West Saxon kings only a brief tenure for 50 years of the southern half of Gloucestershire down to Bath and the Avon, including the part of our present Somerset north of that river, of course, and conceivably the narrow strip between the Avon and Wansdyke. In 628 the Saxon farmers in the areas north of the river were probably not turned out, but transferred to Hwiccia with their land. The real conquest of Somerset must have begun with the battle of 652 at Bradford-on-Avon and the battle of Penselwood in 658, both places on the western edge of Selwood—or else the real conquest must have provoked these reactions, if William of Malmesbury is right in suggesting that the Britons were the aggressors or about to be such, "rebellionem meditantes".

Recognising that in the 75 years after Dyrham the racial frontier, when it did come into existence, was probably no more than an irregular zigzag moving slowly south-westward, progress being due to the spade as much as the sword (or scramasaxe) we can turn now to the military events enlarging the West Saxon kingdom.

CHAPTER TWO

Cenwalh

THE next important name after Ceawlin's is that of Cenwalh, variously spelt Kenwealh, Coinwalch and even Kenwalk, who succeeded his father Cynegils as King of the West Saxons in 643. He started life as a Christian and married the sister of Penda, the formidable King of Mercia. On his accession he abjured Christianity and repudiated his wife, whereupon Penda drove him from his kingdom. During his three years of exile in East Anglia he was brought back to the Christian faith. His nephew Cuthred restored him to his kingdom in 648 and, as a completely reformed character, he at once started to build the Old Minster of St. Peter's at Winchester. He also rewarded his restorer Cuthred with 3000 hides of land in Berkshire.[50]

Bede rather unkindly remarks of this generous benefactor of the Church that he often lost large areas of his kingdom to his enemies, as though it was a sort of habit.[51] He may well have decided that his only chance of adding to his possessions was to go south-west. Penda, after a life full of fighting, was killed in 655, but his son Wulfhere was as powerful and aggressive as his father had been, and on one occasion, after "harrying" in Berkshire, even conquered the Isle of Wight, which he at once gave away. The Mercians of those days seem to have had some resemblance to the Germans of ours, with a maniac fear of "encirclement" and a craze to gain "lebensraum", plus the usual desire to dominate, highly developed.

Under the year 652 the *Anglo-Saxon Chronicle* says, "In this year, Cenwealh fought at Bradford-on-Avon". The cause of the battle is not known, nor is the enemy stated. Albany Major suggests that encroachments by individual settlers might have led to British resentment, culminating in the battle.[52] The Rev. Wm. Hunt says, "William of Malmesbury must refer to this campaign when he speaks of a rising of the Welsh and of a victory gained by the West Saxons at a place called Wirtgernesburg."[53] William's words are quoted later. On the other hand, Ethelwerd says that Kenwalh "fought a battle against his own people, at a place called Bradford, on the river Afene", implying that this was an incident in a civil war or rebellion[54] and, although Ethelwerd is regarded as a "Tenth Century chronicler, full of errors"[55] and is not to be regarded as comparable with William of Malmesbury, he is still a writer of the tenth century, whereas William is writing in the twelfth. Whatever the cause, it is clear that Cenwalh's victory gave him the narrow strip of land, left to the Britons after Dyrham between Malmesbury and Bradford, running beside Braydon and Selwood Forests.[56] This pocket of West Welsh land now became a part of Wessex and as such in 705 came into the new Sherborne diocese "west of the wood" when Ine set it up.[57] It was the Abbot of Malmesbury, Aldhelm, who was made first Bishop of Sherborne (and so of "Selwoodshire", "be Westan Selewuda"). Being a member of the West Saxon royal house, he no doubt had this victory in mind as being worthy of gratitude to God when he built the famous Saxon church in use to-day at Bradford-on-Avon.[58] As a missionary bishop, he must have been aware, too, of the importance to his work of the Avon crossing at Bradford.

The real advance took place in 658, when Cenwalh won a battle at Peonnan or the Pens, a pen being a hill. Under 658 the *Chronicle* records that "In this year Cenwealh fought against the Britons (Welsh) at Peonnan, and put them to flight as far as the Parrett". (His return from East Anglia is mentioned as preceding the battle but it must have done so by ten years.) The place is generally taken to be Penselwood, a tiny village at the south end of a ridge 750 feet high and two miles long, with a camp, marked "castle" on the O.S. map (and in old editions, such as the first, issued in 1817, as "Jack's Castle"), at the north end of it. The village is three miles north-east of Wincanton and exactly one mile from the spot where the counties of Somerset, Wiltshire and Dorset were later to meet and still do so. The camp is believed to have been Cenwalh's. [59] It consists of a great circular bank and ditch covered with old trees, and with a road, which forms the boundary between Somerset and Wiltshire, running through the middle of it: it belongs to the Forestry Commission. The country round about would most aptly be called "the hills". In this place the hills are many and steep and still densely wooded with fragments of the old Selwood Forest. The ancient Hardway or Harrow Way, that crossed Wiltshire and Hampshire and appears in the other direction to have swung south to Yeovil or Sherborne, ran a mile north of the camp. Oddly enough, it was also at Penselwood that Edmond Ironside beat Canute in 1016 and it is only nine miles away that Arthur, it is said, had his chief fortress of Camelot or Cadbury. [60]

William of Malmesbury says that Cenwalh totally defeated "in two actions the Britons, furious with the recollection of their ancient liberty, and in consequence perpetually meditating resistance; first at a place called Wirtgernesburg and then at a mountain named Pene". [61] This clearly indicates that William had read somewhere that, both at Bradford and at Penselwood, the Britons were the aggressors. If so, they must either have felt that Saxon infiltration could no longer be borne or have decided to get their blow in first, before a threatened invasion of mid-Somerset. Two other twelfth-century writers mention the battle of Penselwood, but not that of Bradford. Florence of Worcester says that in 657 Cenwalh fought with the Britons and drove them as far as the Parrett, [62] while Henry of Huntingdon states that the Britons at first had a slight success, but later turned their backs and were driven as far as the Parrett. [63]

Albany Major thinks that, in an undrained Somerset, the Parrett must have covered a very large, ill-defined area with water and therefore that "Pedridan" refers not only to the River Parrett, but also to some specific place upon it, with a name derived from "Pedridan". He prefers South Petherton to Puriton, but it

24

appears that there is no philological argument in favour of this.[64] At the same time, Ethelwerd in the tenth century says that Cenwalh "renewed the war against the Britons and pursued them to a place called Pederydan" (which J. A. Giles calls Petherton in a note)[65] and there is a strong topographical argument. We do not know what was the state of the Roman roads in 658, but if they were not covered with undergrowth—and there is a school of thought which holds that the Fosse Way was not used in Roman times for through traffic after A.D. 47 or 50, when it ceased to be a frontier[66]—it would have been a sensible thing for fugitives from Penselwood to go down the Hardway, thence through the present Sparkford and so to the Fosse Way at Ilchester. If one does this even now, one is able to cross the Parrett at Petherton Bridge, a mile from South Petherton. A guide book says that the stones of the Roman ford here can still be seen in places when the water is down.[67] This would undoubtedly have provided the best means for a hasty retreat, for those who knew of it.

We must not suppose that, when driven to the Parrett, whether they crossed it or not—and we cannot know whether the upper or the lower part of the river is referred to—the West Welsh or Britons stayed there. The days of extermination were over. If the West Saxons were now officially Christians, Birinus, their first bishop, Agilbert of Gaul, his successor, and their helpers had not had long to alter Saxon manners—only from 634 to 658—and the re-conversion of King Cenwalh himself was somewhat new. On the other hand, we are talking of a time when the Conquest was in its closing stages and no one wanted to destroy the labour-force: this battle took place only thirty years before the Laws of Ine gave the Welsh a legal position in West Saxon territory, with the right to hold land. No doubt, after surrendering and handing in their weapons, if they had not run fast enough or far enough, the Britons sneaked quietly back to their homes again. It is doubtful whether many of them did cross the Parrett, apart from those who made off down the Fosse Way to South Petherton: even nowadays below Langport there are bridges only at Burrow Bridge and at Bridgwater. But the days when the fugitives had been subjects of Dyfnaint or Dumnonia (or possibly members of the Durotriges) were gone for ever. Even if the battle of Pensel-wood initiated no great migrations of the Britons out of mid-Somerset, the official boundary, one supposes, was now the Parrett.[68]

Where the Saxons and where the West Welsh predominated in numbers is another matter. Armitage Robinson says, "It does not follow that the whole of Somerset east of the Parrett was at once occupied and held by the English: indeed, the failure of Glastonbury to retain Brent Knoll suggests that at any rate the district near the sea was still debated territory." Note, however, that Abbot Brithwald is said to have deserted or relinquished the land of his own accord.[69]

One British or West Welsh institution Cenwalh and his West Saxons found, and left, in full operation—the monastic church at Glastonbury, already the greatest of the shrines of the Celtic Church and already closely linked with the Church in Ireland.[70] Why, even so early as this, it had its special aura of sanctity, still perceptible to some, it is difficult to say. William of Malmesbury writes "The Ealde Chirche . . . of wattlework, at first, savoured somewhat of heavenly sanctity even from its very foundation and exhaled it over the whole country; claiming superior reverence, though the structure was mean."[71] What is certain is that the wattle church, sixty feet long by twenty-six feet wide, on the exact site of which the ruins of the Lady Chapel stand to-day, and the surrounding huts of the monks were spared by Cenwalh.[72] It is doubtful whether Cenwalh took much notice of Glastonbury until 670, when he realised that the correct, and the pious, thing to do was to present some land to the monastery. He no doubt knew before this what Glastonbury was, for he confirmed the British abbot Bregored in office and this abbot died about 669, to be followed by a Saxon, Beorthwald. The land granted was called Ferramere (Meare and Meare Pool).[73]

The Ealde Chirche, the Vetusta Ecclesia, the Lignea Basilica, variously said on the one part not to have been built by human hands and on the other to have been made by no other hands than those of the disciples of Christ,[74] was preserved until the great fire of 1184, thanks to Paulinus, or perhaps to the teacher of St. David, Paul Hen, who covered it with wooden panelling and with lead from top to bottom.[75] The Great Church of SS. Peter and Paul in its successive forms, from Ine's onwards, was always built or re-built just to the east of it.[76] Hence Celtic and English churches, in their material aspects, existed side by side, and the place became a shrine common to both races.[77] "Glastonbury," says Armitage Robinson, "never ceased to be a centre of Celtic pilgrimage and as a temple of reconciliation must have played no small part in blending the two races."[78] It also continued to be a great link with the Irish Church, possibly, later on, for the wrong reason, that the bones of St. Patrick were erroneously said to have been buried there. It seems that Saxon monks were gradually introduced, but a small area in the town, Beckery, was allotted to Irish pilgrims.[79]

CHAPTER THREE

Centwine

WHEN Cenwalh died in 672, his widow, Queen Seaxburgh, was chosen to succeed him, but she died in the following year and was followed by Aescwine in 674. He died two years later and Centwine, brother of Cenwalh, was chosen King of the West Saxons. In a sense, he had twice been "passed over" for the kingship, but it can hardly have been on account of youth: he reigned for only nine years and then abdicated, dying within the year.[80] With Centwine's reign we enter upon some of the most obscure problems of English history. It is not possible to say where Centwine's work ended and where Ine's began. What is clear is that between them they completed the conquest of Somerset and achieved that of Devon. When Centwine became king, a two-pronged advance into the south-western peninsula was being built up, (as Freeman indicated so long ago as 1874 in his paper on Ine).[81] This idea of two lines of advance, one alongside the Bristol Channel and one alongside the English Channel, is a fundamental one.

The *Anglo-Saxon Chronicle* says of 682, "In this year Centwine put the Britons to flight as far as the sea". This is echoed by Ethelwerd, who says, "After two years King Kentwine drove the Britons out of their country to the sea",[82] by Florence of Worcester (d. 1118), who says that Centwine, King of Wessex, drove the Britons of the West at the sword's point as far as the sea[83] and by Henry of Huntingdon, writing (by his bishop's orders) about 1130. Henry's version is more picturesque but equally an echo of a previous *Chronicle*: "Centwine rex VII anno regni sui congressus est Brittannos, eosque male resistentes, victoriosus et vehemens caede et incendiis ad mare fugavit."[84]

All agree about the date, but, as not one mentions the place, the driving of the Britons to the sea presents a problem. Until fairly recently, writers believed that Centwine's achievement was to drive the Britons out of the land bounded by the Quantocks, the Bristol Channel and the lower Parrett and possibly out of the Quantock Hills as well. J. J. Alexander in 1939 suggested that the drive to the sea was an attack down the Teign and the Dart valleys,[85] but Dr. W. G. Hoskins in 1960 stated his belief that the Britons in 682 were driven to the Atlantic coast near Poundstock, in north-east Cornwall.[86]

Aldhelm, who was not only a saint but a contemporary of Centwine and a member of the West Saxon royal family, describes Centwine as a strong king who ruled the kingdom of Wessex successfully for many years, gave large endowments to newly-formed churches and defeated (unnamed) enemies in three great battles[87] (and Appendix A). These three great battles, all unplaced and undated, seem to demand a shift of emphasis.

If earlier historians did know that Centwine won three great battles, this campaign of 682 must have seemed to them to be a culmination. One is tempted to say that the three battles had a relatively small result, if they were all fought with the same objective of gaining the Quantocks and the land between these hills and the sea. We have no indication whether one or two of the three might have been fought against external enemies, such as the Mercians, or against internal rivals. (There is Bede's mysterious story of the aldermen and the *Chronicle* story of Caedwalla's beginning "to contend for the kingdom".) Centwine must have been a singularly lucky King of Wessex if he had no troubles of these kinds: Ine had plenty.[88] That someone, at some time, enforced Saxon rule on west Somerset and north Devon is obvious, and in advancing from Parrett to Taw there must have been plenty of occasions to produce military incidents, even a great battle or two. There was also the advance from Dorset.

The central fact with which earlier historians have had to cope is Centwine's grant of land at West Monkton (Quantock Wood) to Glastonbury. This shows that the King of the West Saxons in 682 controlled land within three miles of the site of Taunton. That Glastonbury Abbey in the Middle Ages owned land here is proved by no less than five separate statements in the Great Chartulary of the Abbey.[89] The evidence that this land was given by Centwine in 682 is convincing but incomplete, because of an unfortunate error in a date, in the typical Glastonbury manner. Centwine is shown to have granted to Hemgisl, Abbot of Glastonbury, "23 mansiones by a wood called Cantucwdu and 3 cassati in the island by the hill which the British call Cructan and we Crycbeorh" (Creechbarrow at Bathpool) but, most unfortunately, in 672 when Centwine had not yet become king. It is almost certainly an error for 682. William of Malmesbury saw some sort of charter relating to this grant when he was at Glastonbury, and Centwine was mentioned as the grantor. It has been suggested that the correct date of this grant is 678, which appears in relation to another grant of 6 hides, at a place not named, in the paragraph before that about Munacatone, Cantucdun and Crucan, that is, West Monkton, Quantock Wood and Creechbarrow. If 678 is the correct date, it would mean that Centwine had reached West Monkton four years before the battle of 682. The whole matter is very involved, but there seems to be little reason to doubt that Centwine was the king who first had West Monkton at his disposal.[90]

Oman believes that, after Cenwalh's death, little progress westward was made until the time of Ine[91] and that Centwine's victory in 682 was a victory of a weak Wessex over a Dumnonian attempt to regain lost territory. He refers to Bede's definite statement that the aldermen divided Wessex among themselves and so ruled for ten years—improbable enough with Mercia always ready to pounce.[92] "Certainly," says Oman, "no advance of the Saxon border is implied, as some historians seem to have inferred. This was a time of chaos, not of growth".[93] Yet Aldhelm, a contemporary of Centwine, with every opportunity of knowing all there was to know of West Saxon affairs, directly contradicts this view,[94] though there may have been some weak government from 672 to 676 when, first, Cenwalh's widow and, second, Aescwine had short periods as rulers.

Albany Major says that, although the West Saxons drove the Britons as far as the sea, they drew the boundary behind the routed foe from the tidal ford at Combwich, near the mouth of the Parrett, along the line of the later Saxon herepath, or army route, on the low ridge, only 263 feet at its highest, between the Combwich inlet and Cannington Brook and so up to Will's Neck (Wealas or Welshman's Ridge) on the spine of the Quantocks.[95] (These Parrett inlets were probably wider and more swampy before the flood-gates were installed.) He mentions a local tradition of a terrible battle "a little below the spur of the hill on which Aisholt stands, almost at the mouth of a pass, near the source of Cannington Brook at Plainsfield".[96] Rather too much, one feels, has been made by Albany Major, W. H. P. Greswell and Dr. Dobson-Hinton of this line from Combwich to the Quantock ridge. Would any tradition have been handed down to the chroniclers about such an insignificant advance as one from the Parrett to this line? Would any chronicler have called this move driving the Britons to the sea?

The Rev. W. Hunt, who wrote the entries on West Saxon kings for the *Dictionary of National Biography* about 1890, thinks that "Centwine subdued the coast west of the Parrett and made his people masters of the Quantock range".[97]

The Rev. W. H. P. Greswell, who wrote a number of books on Somerset history in the first twenty years of this century, thinks that Centwine, and, later, Ine, advanced by way of Combwich and the lower Parrett along the line of the great Saxon "herepath", or army way (which had not yet been formed or worked out); this, he claims, crossed the Quantocks and ran along the Brendons.[98]

R. H. Hodgkin whose great *History of the Anglo-Saxons* appeared in 1935, thinks that the *Chronicle* entry for 682 means that the country was conquered "at least as far as the Quantocks" and he uses the West Monkton or Quantock Wood grant as a proof. He thinks that there is much to be said for the view that Ine's work in the West of England was chiefly that of consolidation.[99]

E. A. Freeman, writing in the early seventies and expressing his views with all proper caution, may perhaps be called the Founder of the County Boundary School. "In default of direct evidence either way," he says, "we may assume that the boundary of Devon and Somerset, which must mark something, answers pretty well to the conquests of Centwine and Ine".[100]

R. A. Smith in the *Victoria County History* about 1906 says that Ine's conquests of 710 may be marked by the County border as it exists today, and if so the Sumorsaetan must have been in possession of the whole county early in the eighth century.[101] W. G. Hoskins, writing in 1960, says that "the remarkable course of the Devon-Somerset boundary" from the sea to the Blackdowns suggests the moorland conquests of the West Saxons and "some kind of racial frontier".[102]

Albany Major will have none of these theories about the county boundary, but says roundly that the Exmoor part of it is not Saxon, not linguistic and not racial. He believes that the boundary fluctuated according to the legal limits of the Royal Forest of Exmoor, which it was administratively convenient to have in one county only. In 1279 and 1298, he says, there was no exact boundary and it was hardly stabilised by the fourteenth century.[103]

There is also the theory of E. T. MacDermot, put forward in his *History of the Forest of Exmoor*, 1911, that there were two lines of advance. The men of West Somerset would have gone along the north coast and another group from the Exeter area, he thinks, occupied the country south of Exmoor and eventually the northern part of Devon as well. The moorland would then have formed a very wide barrier of wild, uncultivable land between the two groups of West Saxon colonists—indeed, he believes in the "inherent probability" that practically all the forest and parish of Exmoor remained unchanged from 800 to 1800 and most of it until 1900. Unfortunately, his theory about the occupation of north Devon does not tally with the fact that the place-names of north and north-west Devon and of north-east Cornwall strongly suggest that those areas must have been colonised by men from west Somerset.[104]

Of recent writers, J. J. Alexander, probably the greatest of all authorities on the conquest of Devon, suggests, as we have seen, that the drive to the sea was made down the valleys of the Teign and the Dart and that the sea was reached somewhere near Dartmouth.[105] W. G. Hoskins in his book on Devon in 1954 suggests that the battle of 682 was fought in mid-Devon, north of Dartmoor and many miles west of Exeter and that it resulted in the pursuit of the defeated Britons as far as the very edge of the Atlantic, leaving the whole of north and west Devon in English hands. In a later book he suggests that the sea was reached by Poundstock, south of Bude Bay, where for about a dozen miles purely Cornish place-names disappear altogether and purely English ones are used.[106] There appears to be no documentary or archaeological evidence for either of these theories and they leave unexplained the necessities that Ine was under of creating a fort at Taunton and of fighting the battle of 710.

They also leave unexplained the colonisation or conquest of Exmoor and north Devon as far west as Hartland Point. E. T. MacDermot must be right in saying that the West Saxons kept to the coastal fringe and to the edges and valleys of Exmoor, for these were the parts amenable to primitive cultivation. The lands occupied by the colonists from west Somerset, he considers, are now the parishes of Oare, Culbone, Porlock, Luccombe, Stoke, Wootton, Cutcombe, Exford, Winsford and Dulverton. The men from around Exeter—if we can believe in them—would have occupied Brendon, Lynton, Martinhoe, Parracombe, Challacombe, High Bray, North Molton, Twitchem and the two Ansteys.[107] It seems clear that in the middle of the seventh century Devon was a sparsely settled Celtic kingdom.[108]

We do not know where Centwine's three battles were and it is unlikely that all three victories would have been needed on the northern line of advance and none on the southern from Dorset through Exeter. From West Monkton (Quantock Wood) to the present Cornish border and over it the Saxons advanced without leaving any record whatever of their actions. Only the place-names attest their presence, until we find land-grants, possibly from 705 and certainly from 729, when King Aethelheard granted 10 hides in the valley of the Torridge, but these grants are very few indeed. It is clear that right down to north-east Cornwall the Saxon settlers came from west Somerset. The three Editors of *Place-Names of Devon* say definitely, "The nomenclature of north and north-west Devon and of north-east Cornwall strongly resembles that of west Somerset, while that of south or at least of south-east Devon has many points in common with that of Dorset . . . we must believe, therefore, that the north-west and centre of Devon were occupied mainly by settlers advancing from Somerset, while the south and south-east of the county were reached by men from Dorset with different habits of place-nomenclature".[109]   On the whole, the old view that it was Centwine's battle of 682 that brought the Quantock area into Wessex seems to be the right one. Infiltration must have followed on the Exmoor fringes in the way E. T. MacDermot suggests. Can we regard Ine's defeat at Hehil in north-east Cornwall in 722 as the ending of the thrust along the north coast of the south-western peninsula begun by Centwine in 682?

The great Freeman said in 1874 that he had "never been able to find any direct record of the conquest of Devonshire or indeed of that of Dorset", but, with the instinct of the true historian, he suggested tentatively then, what appears obvious now, that "while the West Saxons were fighting their way along the northern coast of the western peninsula, they may have been fighting it with greater speed along the southern coast". Now, however, we are not so sure that they had to fight it out all the way: agricultural infiltration seems to have been possible in the very sparsely populated area Devon is now thought to have been.

The advance of the West Saxons through Dorset, the land of the Durotriges, has received little attention and practically nothing is known about it. W. G. Hoskins has recently called attention to the battle of Beandun, believed to have taken place at the hamlet of Bindon near Axmouth and on the east side of the estuary. (There is another Dorset Bindon, an Iron Age continental "beach head" or landing place, at Lulworth.)[110] The *Anglo-Saxon Chronicle* says under 614, "In this year Cynegils and Cwichelm fought at Beandun and killed 2045 Britons" (Welsh).[111] Presumably the Saxon army consisted of men who were descendants of followers of Cerdic and Cynric, men whose ancestors had landed at Totton on Southampton Water about 495 but had not eventually marched north into Wiltshire about 552. One rather doubts a chronology by which a father and one son were fighting in 614 and another son, Centwine, in 682, so possibly 614 is an incorrect date—in fact, up to 890 all Anglo-Saxon dates should be treated as only the best approximations we have. Cynegils is said to have become king in 611 and to have reigned for 31 years, so it would have been possible for this battle to occur later. It seems impossible to fit the mysterious and possibly mythical second battle of Mount Badon into this advance: it is alleged to have occurred in 665 at Badbury Rings, but few now believe that the first battle with the same name took place there. Nor do we feel able to accept the view of Prof. Hoskins that the battle following Beandun, the battle of Pen, known as Penselwood, in 658 was fought at Pinn Beacon, one and a half miles west of Sidmouth or else at Pinhoe just outside Exeter.[112] This involves the belief that the Britons were driven to the Parrett 25 miles in a north-easterly direction, quite the wrong one. At the same time, it seems odd that we have no evidence that the Saxons were in Exeter until about 680.

Possibly the West Saxon advance from Dorset halted for a time. J. J. Alexander has suggested that the axis of the advance was along the Dorchester–Exeter road, but this is to think in terms of a military operation only instead of a semi-agricultural, gradual occupation of territory. It is quite probable that the West Saxons avoided crossing estuaries at their mouths and that they went upstream to cross the Axe and the Otter, as he says—perhaps through Honiton.[113]

R. H. Hodgkin held the view that a Saxon invasion between 650 and 670 had resulted in the formation of a Saxon enclave of considerable area around Exeter and Crediton, in the valleys of the lower Exe and the Creedy.[114] Although J. J. Alexander says that there are no records of Saxon expeditions made by sea in the seventh and eighth centuries,[115] this is hard to explain unless the invaders did arrive by water.

Exeter is almost unique in having been continuously inhabited from Roman times, but it was almost certainly a poor, insignificant place at this period.[116] It would not be surprising if the entry of the Saxons was peaceable, for it seems clear that a friendly arrangement was made by which the Saxons lived in the south of the town and the West Welsh in the northern half, where the parishes to this day are named after Celtic saints, St. David (hence the name of the railway station), St. Kerian, St. Petrock and St. Sidwell, presumably St. Idwal. It was not until 926 that Athelstan drove the remaining Britons out of Exeter. There was no doubt room for all, especially as many of the West Saxon colonists went on to settle around Crediton in the historic Hundred of Crediton, granted in 739 by King Aethelheard to the Bishop of Sherborne.[117]

J. J. Alexander considers that it is not unlikely that the Exeter neighbourhood was conquered by the West Saxons between 665 and 670, and that by 685 the Crediton area had been occupied, as well as the Honiton area. Curious evidence is furnished by the education of Winfrith, later known as St. Boniface, the Apostle of Germany. There is a tradition that he was born at Crediton[118] and his biographer Willibald, writing about 760, states that when four or five he was fascinated by the teaching of some visiting missionaries and a year or two later (when five or six or seven, that is) went with his father's consent to a monastic school at Exeter. Boniface says himself that he was born "de gente Anglorum" and the abbot of the monastery is said to have been called Wulfhard or Wulfheard, an English name. This has been taken to mean that the monastery was Saxon, but this does not follow: at Glastonbury the Celtic abbot was allowed to remain after 658 but on his death a Saxon was appointed. The Saxon authorities at Exeter may well have put Wulfhard into a Celtic

36

monastery as its ruler, especially if it was in the southern half of the city, now appropriated to English use. Boniface may have developed his racial prejudice against the Welsh here: he certainly was not content with the standard of education available and later moved elsewhere. As Boniface is believed to have been born between 675 and 680, it appears that an English boy from a family settled about seven miles north-west of Exeter entered a monastery school in the city not later than 687 and that the abbot was a Saxon. We cannot say that the monastery was of Saxon foundation but it must have been under a Saxon abbot long enough to send out a mission about 685. According to tradition, no Welsh monastery would have tried to convert the Saxon invaders—but that attitude may have been dying. Possibly the missionaries were minster priests on their ordinary rounds. Prof. Hoskins makes the interesting suggestion that the monastery may have been a daughter-house of Glastonbury, the great Christian foundation of Dumnonia, but he says, of course, that there is no proof of this.[119] He also claims that "Glastonbury, Sherborne and Exeter were all founded or re-founded by Cenwalh, or their endowments increased by him, within the brief period between 670 and 672", but one would like to know what the evidence is.[120] It is most regrettable that for the date of the Saxon arrival at Exeter we have to put all our reliance upon Willibald: the date is the latest possible.

The year 685 was that of Centwine's abdication and it seems undeniable that Centwine, first as a prince, the brother of Cenwalh the King and, like him, the son of Cynegils who had won the battle of Beandun, and then as King, must have taken a chief part in the conquest of the Honiton–Exeter–Crediton area—in addition to whatever he may have done in the Quantock and Exmoor area. At last Centwine is coming into his own: Prof. Finberg even says, "For the true conqueror of Devon we must look back to Centwine".[121] Perhaps the most illuminating remark made on this whole historical problem in recent years is that of J. J. Alexander: "Cenwalh reigned until 672 or 673 and it is not improbable that during his last 12 or 15 years his brother Centwine acted as his deputy in West Wessex, while he himself was watching the Mercians on his northern frontier, and that Centwine's two unrecorded campaigns were the conquest of south Somerset and Dorset about 660 and the conquest of east Devon and Exeter and central Devon as far as Crediton not later than 670".[122] This does not preclude the probability that Centwine fought also in the Quantock neighbourhood, perhaps in 682. Altogether, it appears that Centwine completed the conquest of Somerset and occupied large parts of Devonshire.

His successor, Caedwalla, who reigned from 685 to 688, was, to judge by the *Chronicle* entries, mainly interested in laying waste Kent, but he made a pious end in Rome.

CHAPTER FOUR

Ine

WITH the election of Ine or Ina in 688, Wessex gained a ruler who was not only a great king and a very successful soldier, but a great man, considerably above the stature of the war-leaders who had ruled the West Saxons for the last century. William of Malmesbury calls him "a rare example of fortitude; a mirror of prudence; unequalled in piety".[123] He was chosen over the head even of his own father, Cenred, a subregulus, who loyally accepted the situation. Ine's treatment of Glastonbury would alone have been enough to earn our gratitude. Here, piously leaving unaltered the Old Church of the Britons, the Vetusta Ecclesia, as strengthened and protected by Paulinus or Paul Hen,[124] he caused to be built to the east of it the Great Church of the Apostles S.S. Peter and Paul "for the sake of his brother Mules, whom the Kentish people burnt below Canterbury".[125] According to William of Malmesbury, he built also a chapel at Glastonbury, below the Great Church, with ornaments and vessels requiring 2,640 pounds of silver and "the altar was composed of 264 pounds of gold".[126] To the estates of the Abbey he added land at Pilton, Brent, Sowy (Othery and the Weston Zoyland district)[127] and, apparently, "20 hides close to Tamar" in Cornwall,[128] as well as other lands. At Sherborne Ine created a new diocese for the people living west of Selwood, including those in the strip of land from Malmesbury to Bradford-on-Avon, and he appointed Aldhelm, Abbot of Malmesbury, to be the first bishop. His code of laws gave the conquered Welsh for the first time a definite legal status and recognised their right to hold land. That they were to be second-class citizens made this step forward no less remarkable: there were Saxon second-class citizens, too.

All this was done in the midst of a considerable territorial expansion into Devon and of warfare external and internal. He began by establishing West Saxon supremacy over all the English south of the Thames. Like all West Saxon kings at this time, he had to cope with trouble from Mercia, and when Coelred invaded Wessex, Ine forced him to retreat, after a desperately fought battle at Wodnesbeorg, where the Eastern Wansdyke crosses the Ridgeway near Alton Priors, south-west of Marlborough.[129] It must have been he who was fighting in Cornwall against the Britons in 722. He had to deal with at least two rebellions, one led by two athelings or princes. One, Cynewulf, he slew in 721, but the other, Ealdberht, lived to fight another day. This man caused trouble at Taunton in 722 but Ine killed him in Sussex three years later.[130] Perhaps it was this last episode which finally disgusted Ine with the world and decided him in 725 or 726 to abdicate and to spend what proved to be the last few months of his life in Rome.

The Laws of Ine survived in writing as a supplement to those of Alfred. They were promulgated between 688 and 694 after being made "with the counsel and teaching of his father, his two bishops (of London and Winchester), his aldermen, his Witan and a large assembly of God's servants". Like all early laws, most of them clarified or re-defined or amended custom and dealt with penalties and compensation for wrongs, but others dealt specifically with fluid frontier conditions, in which Saxon landowners were taking more land and reducing it to cultivation among pockets of Welsh who had decided not to leave their lands, but to live beside the invaders and accept the Saxon ruler. They marked the final stages of a long period of conquest and colonisation and show us what, at this late stage, "conquest" had come to mean. To the "Welshman" they gave definite legal rights, recognised him as a permanent, if second-class, citizen and gave him power to own land. They settled a scale of wergilds for the "Welsh" living in Somerset: it was a much lower scale of compensation than that for the murdered or injured Saxons with the same amount of land in their possession, but it was just as definite. "A Welshman, if he has five hides, is a man of six-hundred wergild." "If a Welshman has a hide of land his wergild is 120 shillings (double that of a slave); if, however, he has half a hide, 80 shillings; if he has none, 60 shillings." Whether Ine had a Welsh mother or not, he was no doubt influenced greatly by Christian ideas as to the treatment of subject races: Aldhelm was his constant adviser.

There were also provisions for regulating colonisation, so that the upper classes should not grab much more land than they could cope with properly. "If a gesith-born man moves elsewhere, he may have with him his reeve and his smith and his children's nurse." All other labour, apparently, must be obtained locally. "He who has 20 hides must show 12 hides of sown land when he wishes to leave," and so on, down the scale. [131]

It used to be thought that Ine built Taunton to secure what he had gained by the battle of 710. The classical view was that in that year Ine pushed across the Tone, which, as we have seen, Centwine must have reached and crossed at West Monkton at least by 682, 28 years earlier, [132] that he won a battle against Geraint of Dumnonia somewhere on the Blackdown Hills, and that he thereupon set up a fort at Taunton. [133] If Centwine did achieve in north and south Devon what we believe him to have achieved, it would have been an obvious thing to build a military base in the centre of the south-western peninsula: Taunton is 13 miles from the Bristol Channel and 21 miles from the English Channel. Apart from the need to consolidate past conquests and to create a base for future ones, there must have been plenty of West Saxon subjects, English as well as Welsh, in west Somerset and east Devon who needed keeping in order. Considering how far Ine had gone in a westerly direction by 722, it is essential to revise our views and there is no reason why we should not regard some such date as 690 as the year when Ine turned some sort of village settlement into a royal fort at or close to Taunton. [134] It is odd that its creation would have gone unrecorded if it had not been dramatically demolished in 722.

Exactly what Ine did in building Taunton we cannot say. Probably his fort was a simple matter of earthen banks and ditches and a wooden stockade,[135] "a fence round a timber hall and buildings".[134] Much excavation has been carried out at Taunton Castle, but there is no evidence that Ine's Taunton of the *Anglo-Saxon Chronicle* was on the site later used for the mediaeval Taunton, where the centre of the modern town now is. It is not doubted that Ine built a township in the valley of the Tone and it has even been suggested that Ine used the abandoned British earthwork at Norton Fitzwarren for his fort. No Saxon finds have been unearthed there, and in Taunton itself the sole Saxon relics are a set of three bone gaming pieces. One would have liked to think that Ine's fort stood where Taunton Castle is to-day, but this is only a possibility. Nevertheless, it may still be worth while to point out that the mediaeval castle, the market house and the centre of the town itself are on the south bank of the Tone, the Dumnonian side.[135]

The great battle of 710 seems to have been part of a planned major offensive campaign by Ine, as he had with him his relative Nun (or Nunna or Nothelm), the feudatory King of Sussex, whose services we may suppose to have been demanded. Nun was a subregulus, or ealdorman of royal blood, placed in Sussex by Ine.[136] The place of the battle is not known, but J. B. Davidson (1824–85), who was highly thought-of as a historian of Devonshire, thought it was just above Taunton on the northern slopes of the Blackdown Hills. Forches Corner (ST 184172), three and a half miles south-east of Wellington and on Buckland Hill, has been mentioned. We must not totally neglect the view that the site was near the Tamar on the far side of Devon: this opinion is likely to gain ground as the significance of Ine's activities in Cornwall is realised more widely. A rather tempting idea—but it is no more—is that it may have been somewhere in the South Molton or the Chulmleigh–Hatherleigh area. A victory there would have been very useful.

The Geraint (Gerontius, Gurguntius, Gwent or Gwrgan) against whom Ine and Nun marched forth to war, who disappears from history with this battle, is said to have been respected by the Saxons. Aldhelm, "directed by a synod of his own people," as Bede says,[137] had written a book dedicated to Geraint and the clergy of Dumnonia, *Adversus Errorem Britonum*, urging them to adopt the Roman form of tonsure. (Aldhelm also complained of the contemptuous way in which the Welsh across the Bristol Channel treated the Saxons when they had to meet them, as though they were unclean.) His dedication to Geraint begins, "Domino gloriosissimo occidentalis regni sceptra gubernanti", but this may have been only courtly politeness. Geraint is known also to have granted the Church at Sherborne 5 hides of land at Macuir or Maker by the Tamar, probably in 705, the year in which Ine established the See of Sherborne, with Aldhelm as the first bishop.[138] Whether it was Geraint whose name William of Malmesbury could not read on the charter, ostensibly of 601, granting the mysterious Yneswitrin to Glastonbury, we shall never know: some think that the document was antedated by at least 75 years, perhaps by a complete century.[139] This matter is dealt with later.

Oddly enough, the *Chronicle* does not state, in any of its versions, that the battle was won by Ine and his Saxons. Under 710 it says simply, "And Ine and his kinsman Nun fought against Geraint, king of the Britons". The monk Florence of Worcester (d. 1118), who relied a great deal on the work of the Irish monk Marianus Scotus who wrote still three and a half centuries after Ine's wars, says that in 710 Ina, the warlike king of the Gewissae, and his kinsman Nun, engaged in war with Gwent, king of the Britons, and defeated him and put him to flight.[140] Henry of Huntingdon says that Ine and Nun fought against Gerente, king of Wales. Higebald, a leader, was killed at the start and at the end Gerente with his men turned their faces from the English and, fleeing, left arms and spoil to their pursuers.[141] But he gives no hint that Geraint was killed.

It is going rather far to say, as the Editors of *Place Names of Devon* do, that after this battle there seems to be no later evidence for the existence of an independent Dumnonian kingdom, even if the emphasis is on the word "independent". Apart from the battle of 722 in Cornwall, claimed, rightly or wrongly, as a victory by the Welsh, and even if Ine did make a grant of land by the Tamar, we must consider the view of J. J. Alexander that "although Ine in 710 conquered north Devon and even penetrated into the northernmost tip of Cornwall, the conquest of south Devon remained incomplete until the wars of Cuthred and Cynewulf, half-way through the eighth century".[142] Cuthred fought against the Britons in 743 and 753, and in 757 Cynewulf "often fought with great battles" against them. In 825 "there was a battle at Galford between the Britons (of Cornwall) and the men of Devon" and in 838 at Hingston Down Egbert beat a combined force of the Britons of Cornwall and "a great pirate host" of Danes. It is clear that the Saxon conquest of the very sparsely populated Devon, depleted of its inhabitants by earlier migrations to Brittany, was a relatively easy matter, but it is equally obvious that Devon was not the hard core of Dumnonia: in Cornwall the Welsh race put up the same kind of tough resistance as the Welsh native princes did in the mountains of Snowdonia up to the time of Edward I. Native kings, probably feudatory after 815, are said to have survived into the early tenth century. One, Dumgarth, died in 875.[143]

We must deal now with Ine's activities in Cornwall, first linking his absence from Taunton in 722 with the victory claimed by the West Welsh in that year.

That Ine was fully occupied elsewhere during a part of 722 is fully proved by events at Taunton. The *Anglo-Saxon Chronicle* says of 722: "In this year Queen Aethelburh demolished Taunton, which Ine had built; and the exile Ealdberht went away into Surrey and Sussex, and Ine fought against the South Saxons." Under 725 it states that "Ine fought against the South Saxons and there slew Ealdberht". It will be well to clear up these events at Taunton before dealing with what were almost certainly Ine's activities during his absence. It is the absence that is important, rather than just another rebellion.

It has been said, but upon what evidence the present writer has failed to ascertain, that in 715, the year when Ine fought his desperate battle against the Mercians at Adam's Grave (Woden's Barrow) south of Marlborough, two athelings of the House of Cerdic, Ealdberht and Cynewulf, rebelled against Ine, and that Ine slew Cynewulf.[144] The *Chronicle* knows nothing of this rebellion of 715, nor do Florence of Worcester and Henry of Huntingdon, but the *Chronicle* and Florence both say that Ine slew Cynewulf in 721. Florence says, too, that in 722 Queen Ethelburh levelled to the ground the castle of Taunton built some time before by King Ine, who fought a battle the same year with the South Saxons. He adds that in 725 Ine in a second battle with the South Saxons slew the Atheling Aldbriht (Ealdberht) whom he had previously driven out of Wessex. It is Henry of Huntingdon, however, (whom Oman thinks to be right "for once") who makes a connected and comprehensible story of Ealdberht's adventures, though he tells the story backwards, beginning in 725 with Ine's killing of the Atheling in a war against Sussex. The Prince had previously been driven from Taunton, which Ine had built; because Ealdberht had entered the castle, Ethelburh the Queen, Ine's wife, had recaptured the castle by force and destroyed it, compelling the atheling to flee into Surrey and Sussex.[145] Queen Ethelburh clearly destroyed the fort, probably consisting of earthen banks and ditches and a wooden stockade surrounding timber buildings, to prevent it from falling into, or more likely, remaining, in rebel hands. She may have had the place set on fire. Demolition was the sensible thing when the main military resources were far away and fully occupied.

Henry of Huntingdon was writing four centuries after this episode at Taunton, but it almost looks as though he had access to some chronicle containing rather fuller information than others. What exactly does he mean by "Ealdbriht castrum introierat, qui regius hostis erat"? Is he hinting or saying that there was a disloyal royal garrison who let the rebel atheling into the fort? Albany Major has a theory that the garrison of Taunton consisted of South Saxons who had enlisted under the banner of Wessex when Wulfhere of Mercia overran their land in 661: if so, they would, or might, have been on Ealdberht's side, for it was in Surrey and Sussex that his supporters were. But this was 60 years after any exodus likely to have taken place from Sussex— a long time. However, "the sporadic occurrence of distinctive Sussex customs in the Manor of Taunton Deane," says Albany Major, supports this belief.

Freeman, in order to explain Ine's absence at this critical time, suggests that the king was absent in Wales, trying to push the Welsh back. This is a quite brilliant suggestion, but cannot be right. The modern Gloucestershire had been absorbed into Hwiccia almost a century ago and the safety of its western frontier was the business of Mercia, not of Wessex.[146] Aethelbald of Mercia, who became king in 716, did apparently have trouble with the Welsh: two battles in 722 in Glamorganshire were claimed as victories by the Welsh and, says Oman, "their enemies can only have been Mercians". They are mentioned as having taken place at Gartmailauc and at Pencon, which are interpreted as Garth-maelog and Pencoed, the latter about four miles east of Bridgend on the main road.[147] That these battles took place in 722 is stated in the *Annales Cambriae*, written about A.D. 1000.

Ine in 722 was fighting against the Welsh, but they were the West Welsh of Cornwall: Freeman was not very far out. The same entry for that year in the *Annales Cambriae* states that the Britons won another battle over the Saxons at Hehil in Cornwall; the man most likely to have been the Saxon leader was Ine himself. (As long ago as 1910 Oman was asking whether this battle might not have been against Ine.) This is evidence of the first importance.

The entry is as follows:

"722 CCLXXVIII Annus. Beli filius Elfin moritur et bellum Hehil apud Cornuenses; gueith Gartmailauc, cat Pencon apud dextrales Brittones; et Brittones victores fuerunt in istis tribus bellis."[148]

"Gueith" signifies bellum and that word is used in MS. C, which adds "Iwor existente duce eorum." It would not have been impossible for Iwor to be leading armies on both sides of the Bristol Channel in the same campaigning season, but it seems unlikely. On the other hand, one Rodri Makvunog of Wales is said to be on record, presumably in the Brut y Tywsogion, as having fought in the Hehil battle.[149]

Whether this battle at Hehil was in fact a West Welsh victory is not so certain. The Rev. Wm. Hunt, who wrote about Ine and other Saxon kings in the *Dictionary of National Biography*, says, "Personally it is evident that Ine had some close relations with the Welsh, who seem to adopt his exploits as those of their legendary hero, Ivor, turning English victories under Ine into Welsh victories under Ivor".[150] From one point of view this does not matter. It would, so far as the conquest of Devon is concerned, be sufficient to know with certainty, if we could, that the Saxon conquest had gone so far into the South-West that Ine found it necessary to fight a battle in Cornwall. Certainty, here, seems almost to have been reached. It seems clear, too, that the battle of Hehil brought to a full stop the West Saxon advance, starting on the Parrett in 682, through west Somerset and north and north-west Devon into north-east Cornwall.

Hehil has been variously identified: it is thought by some to be either Hayle, at the head of St. Ives Bay, or the Camel Estuary, the old name of the river having been Hehil or Haegel. This second suggestion supports the idea that the battle against Geraint in 710 gave Ine north Devon. To Ine, if he was pushing on down the coast, the Camel estuary at Padstow would have been the next great obstacle: to the Welsh it would have seemed that, if Ine was allowed to go further, all would be lost. A third suggestion, made in *Place Names of Devon*, is that a hamlet called Hele in Jacobstow near Poundstock was the site. It is two and a half miles from the sea and on or near a linguistic or place-name frontier. A fourth idea, and the most acceptable in many ways, is that supported by J. J. Alexander, Preb. Melhuish and C. Henderson in favour of Hele Bridge, nearly two miles south of

Bude and close to Whalesborough or Walesbrewe, "the fortress of the Welsh". Alexander claimed that the River Bude from Jacobstow downwards was a national frontier, with "scarcely a Celtic farm name to the east of the stream, although Tre, Pol and Pen are common enough in Poundstock and Jacobstow". The linguistic frontier, he and Prof. Hoskins think, ran down the Ottery to the Tamar.[151]

The other piece of evidence used to prove Ine's presence in Cornwall needs handling with the greatest care and, indeed, the greatest scepticism. This is the alleged grant of land next to the Tamar to Berwald, who was abbot of Glastonbury between 705 (possibly 702) and 712. This must be mentioned and, if mentioned at all, it can be dealt with only by going into minute details. We may as well repeat at once that Alexander does not believe that the valleys of the Plym, the Tavey and the Lower Tamar were reached until the wars of Cuthred and Cynewulf between 753 and 765.[152]

It must also be said that the only land in Cornwall belonging to Glastonbury to receive mention in the Great Chartulary of the Abbey is Lamana or Lammana, which is Looe Island, also called St. George's Island, and a piece of the mainland opposite. There is no charter of grant, but incidental references are absolutely conclusive that for a period the monastery owned this property. There are even remains of buildings that formed a "cell" of the Glastonbury monastery. The property was ultimately alienated, as we know from a fourteenth century pencil note by a scribe at the end of Charter No. 1066. The Great Chartulary is a fourteenth century manuscript compiled for practical purposes, and we are dealing with property that may have belonged to Glastonbury at or after the beginning of the eighth century and may later have been lost in early wars, sold or exchanged—perhaps exchanged after a war, an island being most suitable for the contemplative life. The fact that a property is not mentioned in the Great Chartulary is not proof that the monastery never possessed it.[153]

Next, William of Malmesbury records that he saw at Glastonbury a charter by which a King of Dyfnaint (or Dumnonia), whose name was indecipherable, in 601 granted the estate of

Yneswitrin to "the Old Church which is situated there". The monks naturally thought that these were title deeds to Glastonbury itself and that Yneswitrin was the Celtic name of Glastonbury.[154]

William of Malmesbury states in *De Antiquitate* that Ine gave Berwald, Abbot of Glastonbury from 705 to 712, 20 hides "by Tamer". This might have been, but is not at all likely to have been, after the battle of 710.[155] Adam of Domerham records a grant by Ine to Berwald in 705 of 20 hides "juxta Tamar" (mentioned in one place first), 20 hides in Bouelt, 12 in Sowy (Zoy), 5 in Corregs (Croscombe), half a hide with fishing rights in Escford and 20 hides in Doulting. Elsewhere a very similar list, not identical, mentions 20 hides at Pilton and 20 at Brent Marsh. In two places in the same work the land next to the Tamar is said to be Linig or Linis (once above the line "in another hand").[156] It does not matter much whether it was or not, seeing that Linig has disappeared from the map, but it is thought to have been in the area between the River Lynher and the Tamar.[157] The place called Ince, which now boasts a castle, on the left bank of the Lynher and two and a half miles south-west of Saltash Bridge, has been suggested, and the further idea has been put forward that Ince is Ynys, the Welsh for island or peninsula, which latter it is.[158] Hence, it is argued, it is that Ynyswitrin which was granted by the King of Dyfnaint in 601 or 701, or whatever one decides. If Geraint, Ine's opponent in 710, was the grantor, Ine would only have been confirming a grant previously made by someone else, but could he have done this in 705 before winning the battle of 710? Possibly he could, if that battle was in north Devon, but there is a stronger objection.

What makes this all the more odd is that Geraint, probably also in 705, the year in which it was made a bishop's see by Ine, granted 5 hides at Macuir or Maker to the church at Sherborne.[159] Maker parish is just across the river from Ince, one might say. This area around the place where the Lynher enters the Tamar has an odd history and seems to have been a constant resource for royal grants, for instance, part of King Egbert's 18 hides to

Sherborne,[160] and it was not until 1844 that 1451 acres of the parish of Maker, west of Plymouth Sound, were transferred from Devon to Cornwall.[161]

The only Lini or Liney in the Glastonbury Chartulary is a part of Weston Zoyland, itself a part of that Sowy which is mentioned in the same list as the land "juxta Tamar".[162]

There is yet another source of doubt, the glaring similarity of two lists of grants, one beginning with land by the Tamar and one beginning with land by the Tan or Tone. 705 is the year given by Birch as the date of another charter of Ine granting land to Berwald, the abbot of Glastonbury mentioned by William of Malmesbury as being elected in 705 and as being granted 20 hides beside Tamar by Ine (though William does not specifically mention the date of grant). It begins with the grant of twenty hides (the same number as by the Tamar) next to the river which is called Tan (Tone) and then goes on to give land at Pouelt (between Othery and Greinton, spelt elsewhere Rouelt and Bouelt), Doluting (Doulting) and Corregescumb (Croscombe)— the familiar names. It does not make mention, as the other list does, of Sowy, nor does it, unnecessarily, mention Pilton separately from Doulting or the half-hide and fishing rights at Escford. Obviously there has been some shocking muddle over the first item. Should Tamar in the other list be Tan or should Tan in this charter be Tamar? Birch says the word is Tau in the facsimile version A, Tan in S and Tamar in Migne's edition of *De Antiquitate*—but the last is hardly evidence.[163] Professor Finberg gives 705 or 706 as the date, preferring 706 for a reason given, and stars this charter as one "Available only in later copy, authenticity not in doubt".[164] It is impossible to identify any Glastonbury land by the Tone except West Monkton and Creechbarrow, but there is no reason why land should not have been given beside that river, as much as by the Tamar—indeed, a grant by the Tone is the more likely—and there is no reason why all traces of later ownership should not have been lost in one case as in the other. This charter might, like the grant of Brent, have been a confirmation of ownership. A difficulty is that 20 hides are mentioned here and

23 in Centwine's grant, with 3 hides at Creechbarrow south of the Tone in addition. This need be no fatal objection, if hides varied in area from district to district and were essentially fiscal units: a reduction in nominal hidage by a new charter would have been a way of making a slight remission in taxation. A scribe, of course, in referring to the West Monkton estate might conceivably have thought that it was 23 hides less 3 across the river.

The way in which these charters semi-duplicate one another and the muddle over the name of the first item make one feel that these copies, and these copies of copies, are none of them to be trusted. The Glastonbury monks seem to have gone in for forging legal documents in a big way and to have been thoroughly inefficient at the job, but no doubt one should distinguish between charters and chartularies. Armitage Robinson takes a more lenient view.

If the land granted was by the Tamar after all and it is the word Tan that is the error and if the date was 705 or 706, as Prof. Finberg feels sure, then we are faced with the fact that the battle of 710 had not been fought when the grant was made, or, if fought, has been wrongly dated. In one way, a grant of land to a monastery in south Cornwall would seem to indicate a secure hold on the country there and make it all the more likely that a battle necessary in 710 was necessary only by the north coast. Could it have been that the monks were unwisely granted land somewhere by the Tamar in 706, possibly in thanksgiving for conquests made, that they or their agent and tenants were thrust out by the Welsh after the Saxon defeat at Hehil in 710, and that they were given Lamana instead when at last the Saxons had reversed the situation?

Altogether, one feels extremely sceptical about this alleged grant by the Tamar—and there is one final question. Why, with all his pious and noble generosity to Glastonbury, did Ine give it no land in Devon? It was not until 729 that a Saxon king made a first grant to Glastonbury of land in Devon; this was when Aethelheard granted 10 hides in the valley of the Torridge.[165] If Ine gave none in Devon, why should he have been likely to be in a position to grant land in Cornwall?

Conclusion

To sum up, it appears that the battle of Dyrham in 577, apart from dividing the enemies of the Saxons for ever and giving the West Saxons a permanent security in Wiltshire, on the other side of Selwood, had little to do with the conquest of Somerset. This seems, in spite of the advent of new theories, to have begun with the battle of 652 at Bradford-on-Avon and that of 658 at Penselwood, whether the Britons were the aggressors or not. With all due deference, the present writer feels unable to accept the view that the second battle was fought at Pinn Beacon near Sidmouth or at Pinhoe outside Exeter, ending with a driving of the Britons 25 miles to the Parrett in a north-easterly direction. Neither does he believe that the victory at Penselwood carried the West Saxons at least as far as the hills between Somerset and Devon, or that the whole of Devon was conquered during the reign of Ine. The first idea carries the Saxons along too fast and the second too slowly.

The driving of the Britons to the sea by Centwine in the Quantock district in 682 now appears to have been part of a two-pronged attack on the Britons of the West, one advance being parallel with the north coast and the other along the south from Dorset to Exeter and so to Crediton and beyond. The conquest of Exmoor and of north Devon must have been initiated by Centwine in his last three years. First as a prince, the brother of King Cenwalh, and then as King, he must also have had much to do with the continuation of the work of his father, Cynegils, at the battle of Beandun (which may well have taken place later than 614) by pushing along the south coast in south-eastern Devon. The advance to Exeter and Crediton may have preceded an advance to the sea between the valleys of the Teign and the Dart, as J. J. Alexander suggests, but why, if this happened, did the Saxons not go on along the south coast to the Tamar until the wars of Cuthred and Cynewulf between 753 and 765, as Alexander believes they did not? As to the battle of Posentesbyrig, if it was fought at Posbury, that would mean that the Crediton area was in the hands of the Saxons in 661, considerably—perhaps 15 years—before we had expected it, but one could possibly believe this. But was it a victory anyhow?[166] Even if it was, it does not follow that the rush to the sea in 682 was from Crediton to Poundstock.[167] Neither does Alexander's advance between the Teign and the Dart valleys preclude the classic doctrine that Centwine conquered the Quantock–Parrett area.

Centwine's three great unnamed battles must have produced immense effect. In fact, it becomes clear that the final success of the two-pronged movement into Devonshire must have owed more to Centwine with his three victories than to anyone else. When he abdicated, the West Saxons must have had a sure footing in the eastern half of Devon, north and south. Ine's battle of 710 must have completed what Centwine had begun by overthrowing Dumnonian authority in Devon, but it was not a fatal blow: the Welsh spirit was unbroken, and when Ine reached north Cornwall, he was stopped and defeated at Hehil in 722. That was the end of the advance from the Parrett along the north coast.

The conquest of Cornwall is another and a very different story and took over a century more: even then, there were native kings, probably vassals of the Kings of England, until the beginning of the tenth century. The separateness of Cornwall was for a thousand years a feature of English life, and its Celtic language, diverging from the Welsh of Wales, lasted until the seventeenth century. The eldest son of the Sovereign is by immemorial custom created Prince of Wales, but the title is all. He is born Duke of Cornwall, with a special endowment of wide lands controlled by his own Council.

Our subject is full of difficulties and it does look as though the historian will never have more material to work upon than he already has. More facts—and one wonders whether we have more now than three or four—are unlikely to emerge, but we can hope for interesting new ideas, such as those of Prof. Finberg and Prof. Hoskins, to be applied to what is on record. The real trouble is that the records are, all of them, of most doubtful reliability. We have to get along with the chronology of the *Anglo-Saxon Chronicle* for events two centuries before it was started, because we have none better. The archaeologist so far has been able to afford little help to the historian of this period of West Country history. It is possible that the spade, perhaps by unearthing one or two more Saxon cemeteries with features more easily interpreted than those of Camerton and Cannington, will provide a few solid facts as to what could prove an interesting conflict between two races. A brief appendix gives a list of the chief archaeological finds. Finality will never be reached, for all historians are in time superseded and the study of History is of the nature of a debate.

Abbreviations

Original Authorities:

A. of D.	Adam of Domerham: *Historia de Rebus Glastoniensibus* (including William of Malmesbury: *De Antiquitate Glastoniensis Ecclesiae*), ed. T. Hearne, Oxford, 1727.
A.-S. C.	*The Anglo-Saxon Chronicle,* translated and edited by D. Whitelock, D. C. Douglas and S. I. Tucker, London, 1961. Also used: Edition of G. N. Garmonsway, Everyman Library, London. Edition of 1954.
Bede, E. H.	Bede: *History of the English Church and People,* translated by L. Sherley Price. Penguin Books, 1955.
Ethelwerd	Ethelwerd's (Aethelweard's) "Chronicle", in *Six Old English Chronicles,* ed. J. A. Giles, London, 1896.
E.H.D. I	*English Historical Documents,* Vol. I, ed. D. Whitelock, London, 1955.
Flor. of Worc.	*Florence of Worcester, Chronicle of.* Translated from Latin by Thomas Forester, London, 1854.
G.C.	*The Great Chartulary of Glastonbury,* ed. Dom Aelred Watkin. 3 Vols. Somerset Record Society, 1947 et seq.
Gildas	"The Works of Gildas and Nennius", translated from Latin by J. A. Giles, London, 1841. Re-printed with a few notes, in *Six Old English Chronicles,* translated by J. A. Giles, London, 1896.
Hy of Hunt.	Henry of Huntingdon: *Historia Anglorum,* ed. T. Arnold. Rolls Series. London, 1879.
Wm of M: De Ant.	William of Malmesbury: "De Antiquitate Glastoniensis Ecclesiae", trans. as *The Antiquities of Glastonbury* by F. Lomax, London. No date, but after 1906.
Wm of M.: De Gestis R.	William of Malmesbury: "De Gestis Regum Anglorum", trans. and ed. J. A. Giles as *Chronicle of the Kings of England.* London, 1876. There is a fine edition in the original Latin, ed. by Bishop Stubbs, in the Rolls Series. London, 1887.
Wm of M.: De Gestis P.	William of Malmesbury: *De Gestis Pontificum Anglorum.* Lib. V ed. N.E.S.A. Hamilton. Rolls Series. London, 1870.

55

Secondary Authorities:

Albany Major: E. W. of W.   Albany Major: *Early Wars of Wessex*, ed. C. W. Whistler. Cambridge, 1913.

Alexander: D.A. 1939   J. J. Alexander: "Tenth Report on Early History (of Devon)". *Transactions of Devonshire Association*, LXXI, 1939.

Alexander: D.A. 1940   J. J. Alexander: "Eleventh Report on Early History (of Devon)". *Transactions of Devonshire Association*, LXXII, 1940.

D.N.B.   *Dictionary of National Biography.*

Finberg: D. and C.   H. P. R. Finberg: *Early Charters of Devon and Cornwall.* Leicester, 1954.

Finberg: Lucerna   H. P. R. Finberg: *Lucerna*. London, 1964.

Finberg: Wessex   H. P. R. Finberg: *Early Charters of Wessex.* Leicester, 1964.

Freeman: Ine I   E. A. Freeman: "King Ine, Part I". *Proceedings of Somerset Archaeological and Natural History Society*, 1872.

Freeman: Ine II   E. A. Freeman: "King Ine, Part II". *Proceedings of Somerset Archaeological and Natural History Society*, 1874.

Grinsell: Arch. of W.   L. V. Grinsell: *The Archaeology of Wessex.* London, 1958.

Hodgkin: Hist. of A.-S.   R. H. Hodgkin: *History of the Anglo-Saxons,* Vol. I. Oxford, 1935.

Hoskins: Devon   W. G. Hoskins: *Devon.* London, 1954.

Hoskins: West Exp. of W.   W. G. Hoskins: *The Westward Expansion of Wessex.* Leicester, 1960.

Hoskins & Finberg: D.S.   W. G. Hoskins and H. P. R. Finberg: *Devonshire Studies.* London, 1952.

Oman: Eng. before N.C.   Sir Charles Oman: *England before the Norman Conquest.* London, 1910.

P.N.D.   *Place Names of Devonshire,* Part I, ed. J. E. B. Gover, A. Mawer and Sir F. Stenton. Cambridge, 1931.

P.S.A.N.H.S.   *Proceedings of the Somerset Archaeological and Natural History Society.*

Stenton: A.-S. Eng.   Sir F. Stenton: *Anglo-Saxon England.* Oxford, 1943.

V.C.H.   *Victoria County History of Somerset.*

Other works are mentioned in full.

Notes and References

1. A.-S. C., p. 14. Possibly the three towns had been strongholds or "Chesters" of Aurelius Caninus or Conanus, the probable descendant of Ambrosius Aurelianus and his successor locally. He was one of those western princes damnated by Gildas. *See* Oman: Eng. before N.C., p. 234.

   Hy of Hunt., p. 53 refers to Gloucestre et Cirecestre et Badecestre. He alludes also to the deaths of "tres reges Christianorum".

   Miss Vera I. Evison in her book, *The Fifth-Century Invasions South of the Thames* (University of London: The Athlone Press, 1965), basing her views on Frankish grave-goods found in England (brooches, swords, shield-bosses, belt-buckles and fittings and so on), holds that the area south of the Thames, from Kent to Hampshire, was conquered, after a number of simultaneous landings in A.D. 449, in one major concerted operation, planned and led by Franks from north-eastern Gaul (Belgium and N.E. France).

   In an ingenious argument she criticises the chronology of the *Anglo-Saxon Chronicle* and suggests that the dates of Ceawlin's reign were 495–528, and that the battle of Fethanleag may well have been the same as the battle of Mons Badonicus and fought in 519. What she does not do is to mention, let alone fit in, the battle of Dyrham. The battle of Bedford took place, she thinks, in 506. According to the *Chronicle*, Dyrham, the Saxon victory, was fought six years later, so giving us 512, according to her system of chronology—seven years before Mons Badonicus, the Saxon defeat, instead of at least 60 years after it.

   We can only straighten things out, if we follow Miss Evison, by suggesting that Dyrham was fought about 512 and was of no real significance because reversed in 519 at Mons Badonicus (Fethanleag), followed by a long period of peace, as Gildas says (possibly ended by the battle of Barbury, which the *Chronicle* puts in 556, but, if so, not under the leaders it gives). However, the *Chronicle* mentions Ceawlin no less than nine times, so that at present it seems difficult to accept this new view of the period of his reign and the implied change of the date of Dyrham. It is, of course, illogical to reject the dates in the *Chronicle* and then to base theories on the intervals between them, but they may give an indication of the sequence of events.

2. No one would claim that the chronology of the *Anglo-Saxon Chronicle* is faultless, but the chroniclers no doubt made use of earlier annals, as well as oral tradition, for the years before 890. For the seven different texts of the *Chronicle* and their relationship, *see* P. Hunter Blair: *An Introduction to Anglo-Saxon England*. Cambridge, 1962, pp. 352–355.

   Stenton in A.-S. Eng., p. 31 says "the traditions preserved in the *Chronicle* are only memoranda derived from verse in praise of ancient kings", but some primitive races, e.g. the Maoris, without writing have retained accurate and detailed information for very long periods by constant repetition.

   For the minstrel's world *see* Widsith (p. 75) and Deor (p. 79) in *Anglo-Saxon Poetry*, ed. R. K. Gordon (Dent's Everyman Library).

57

3. This movement was not, as used to be thought, the origin of the sub-kingdom of Hwiccia. Stenton thinks that the West Saxons occupied the lower Severn basin for half-a-century after 577. The middle Severn area of Worcestershire and Warwickshire was probably colonised by Middle Anglians from the valleys around the Wash and by West Saxons from the Upper Thames. After the defeat inflicted on the West Saxons by Penda (as yet possibly an adventurer fighting for his own ends) at Cirencester in 628 and on the terms made there, Penda probably united these people under himself. Later, of course, he became King of Mercia. Stenton: A.-S. Eng., pp. 44 and 45.

Luckily we do not need to decide how far north Ceawlin went up the Severn Valley. The battle of Fethanleag is a fine subject for the student of historiography. Its site was first believed to be at Fretherne, 8 miles S.W. of Gloucester (a sensible idea), then at Faddiley near Nantwich in Cheshire, and now the view is that it was near Stoke Lyne, just north of Bicester in Oxfordshire. Equally varied accounts have been given of the result.

4. H. P. R. Finberg: *Lucerna*, p. 89, Note 1 states that the kings may at one time have ruled on both sides of the Severn Sea. Reference made to *Studies in Early British History*, ed. N. K. Chadwick, p. 53, Cambridge. Hence Aldhelm's complaint to Geraint of the way in which the Welsh of Wales treated travelling Saxons.

5. For this battle we have the irrefragable contemporary evidence of Gildas in his *De Excidio et Conquestu Britanniae*, written about 545. (It has been "improved" by mediaeval scribes but not thereby ruined). Gildas mentions Ambrosius by name (p. 22, §§ 25 and 26 in edn. by Giles) but not Arthur. Bede copies Gildas in E.H.

If Mount Badon (Mons Badonis, Mons Badonicus) was fought in or about 500, the Britons were probably led by Ambrosius Aurelianus, who emerged about 472, but possibly by Arthur. If the battle took place about 517—and the Welsh date is 516, given in Annales Cambriae, with a mention of Arthur by name—the British leader was probably Arthur; Ambrosius would have been too old.

The historic existence of Arthur can never be proved, but there is still a chance that archaeology may shed some light. Typical comments of modern historians are these:

Prof. K. H. Jackson: "Nothing is certain about the historical Arthur, not even his existence." (*Arthurian Literature in the Middle Ages*, ed. R. S. Loomis. Oxford, 1949, Ch. 1 on "The Arthur of History").

The late Prof. R. G. Collingwood: "The historicity of the man can hardly be called in question." (*Roman Britain and the English Settlements*, by himself and J. N. L. Myres. Oxford, 1936, p. 321.)

Prof. Thomas Jones: "Nothing is known about him as a historical character, although his existence can no longer be denied." (Article in *Dictionary of Welsh Biography*.)

The battle probably took place at Liddington "Castle", an Iron Age fort 4 miles S.E. of Swindon and 4½ miles from a village called Baydon, a fact seldom mentioned. Other sites favoured are Badbury Hill, near Farringdon, Badbury Rings in Dorset and Whitsbury Camp above Charford. Early antiquaries believed that a hill outside Bath was the place.

6. Stenton: A.-S. Eng., p. 7. The story of the return to Germany of the scared Anglo-Saxons was written down by a monk of Fulda, about

60 miles N.E. of Frankfurt, about 865. Ancestors of some Saxons then on the Continent were descended from Angli from Britain, who, compelled to find new land, had crossed the sea and landed at Haduloha, the modern Cuxhaven, at the mouth of the Elbe. A Frankish King, Theuderich, invited their help in the Thuringian War, and after it gave these immigrants from Britain some land he had conquered with their help, north of the river Unstrut. This war can be precisely dated at 531, 30 years after the early date for Mount Badon and 14 years after the later one.

Procopius of Caesarea, writing in Constantinople about 560, said that there were in Britain Angles, Frisians and Britons, and that they were so numerous that numbers of them emigrated to France every year. One King of the Franks on sending an embassy to Constantinople included some Angles in the party as prestige symbols, "making display, as if the island also was ruled by him." ("Gothic War Bk. IV", Cap. 20, quoted in R. W. Chambers: *England before the Norman Conquest*, 1928, p. 100.) This sounds like truth.

7. G. M. Trevelyan: *History of England*. London, 1926, p. 40.

8. Gildas, p. 22 §26.

9. Grinsell: Arch. of W., p. 278.

10. A.-S.C., Annal 571. *See* also Note 3 above.

11. V.C.H. Som., Vol. II. Chapter on "Political History", by M. A. W. Sandford, p. 175.

12. W. J. Wedlake: *Excavations at Camerton, Somerset*. Camerton Excavation Club, 1958, p. 96.

13. D. P. Dobson-Hinton: *Archaeology of Somerset*. London, 1931, p. 180.

14. L. V. Grinsell: Arch. of W., p. 280 and p. 293. G. J. Copley considers that nothing at Camerton need have been earlier than the Conversion, and doubts whether interment at Buckland was any earlier than at Camerton. (*The Conquest of Wessex in the Sixth Century*, 1954, p. 69.) A new theory is that the Camerton cemetery may have been started in the Roman period. L. V. Grinsell mentions this idea in P.S.A.N.H.S., 1965, p. 64.

15. Albany Major: E. W. of W., p. 25 says, "Apart from possible encroachments on the country between the Avon and the Mendips, for which there is nothing beyond theory, there was no attempt on the part of the West Saxons to extend their conquests to the West or to challenge the power of Dyvnaint". He also says, p. 24, that the actual frontier to the south of the Saxon territory was marked by the Wansdyke. (This, of course, is opinion, not proof.)

16. That the Western Wansdyke did start west of Maes Knoll has been more or less established. A deed of the reign of Edward II (A.D. 1310) mentions Wondesditch Lane, near Yanley, Long Ashton. *See* Grinsell: Arch. of W., p. 284 and his reference to Sir Richard Colt Hoare: *Ancient Wilts*, ii. 20–21. This view is not accepted by Sir Cyril and Lady Fox or by Dr. J. N. L. Myres.

A. G. C. Turner in P.S.A.N.H.S., 1951, p. 152 says the first element in "Marksbury" is Old English ME(A)RC, mark, sign, boundary, frontier, limit and that the Wansdyke may have been the boundary between the Saxons and the Britons. He and G. B. Grundy think that the village of Marksbury received its name from the ancient earthwork on Stantonbury Hill, into which, and out of which the Wansdyke runs. This earthwork is described as Merces Burh in 941, i.e. as a boundary fort. When the village appropriated the name of the earthwork, a new name had to be found for the latter, and it took it from the village of Stanton Prior just below it.

Ekwall has other views: he thinks Marksbury was the fort of a man called Maerec.

17. Sir Cyril and Lady Fox: "Wansdyke Reconsidered", *Archaeological Journal*, CXV for 1958, published 1960.

18. Stenton: A.-S. Eng., p. 45.

19. The Fox theory states that Wansdyke was intended by the Saxons to prevent invasion, and control or prevent traffic from Mercia down the Fosse Way from 628 onwards, just as Grim's Ditch was intended to prevent invasion down the Icknield Way in the Chilterns. This implies that the Saxons had occupied enough of north and central Somerset to make it worth guarding, but there is no real evidence of this for another 30 years. Would anybody have built a bank from Portbury to the southern outskirts of Bath merely in order to "enfilade" the Fosse Way? There was, however, a ford at Saltford.

That Marksbury is so called is a fact that can be used in two ways: Saxons might have called it that whether looking north at the Mercians or looking south at the Britons, in accordance with the usual view.

A. G. C. Turner does say that "place names containing Celtic elements are rare to the north of Wansdyke, but become more common to the south of it". (P.S.A.N.H.S., XCV, 1951, p. 152, Note 2). This seems to reinforce the ordinary view.

It is a reasonable hypothesis that the two Wansdykes were built at different periods, the Western after 577 (or 628) and the Eastern pre-Badon. As the Eastern has been raised at some time, it may have been used not only for the Britons pre-Badon, but by the Saxons advancing over Salisbury Plain, between the capture of Old Sarum in 551 and the battle of Barbury in 556. This increase in height would hardly seem worth the trouble, until one remembers the unbelievable amount of digging in World War I, done by millions compared with the Saxons' thousands, but in the most dangerous conditions the world has seen.

J. N. L. Myres in 1964 stated "a strong case for believing that the West and East Wansdykes were constructed at one period and for one purpose". (L. V. Grinsell: P.S.A.N.H.S., 109, 1965, p. 64.)

20. V.C.H. Som., Vol. I, 1906, Chapter on "Anglo-Saxon Remains" by R. A. Smith, p. 374. "So far then there are some slight indications that the Saxons did not occupy in force the territory they had conquered, at any rate beyond the Bristol Avon, though the land immediately to the south of Bath no doubt passed into their hands with the Roman city; and archaeological researches lend support to the theory that for three parts of a century the Saxon territory was here bounded to the south by the earthwork known as Wansdyke." Woden was the god of boundaries and "Wansdyke" is "Woden's Dyke". Did the man buried at Buckland Dinham cross the boundary? *See* Appendix B.

Penda did not become King of Mercia until 632. Stenton: A.-S. Eng., pp. 44 and 45, but the Laud (E) version of A.-S. C. says he became King in 626. See also Note 15, and the Parker (A) version suggests the same.

21. L. V. Grinsell: Arch. of W., p. 279.

22. One prehistoric trackway runs from the chalk of the Wiltshire Downs through Chapmanslade and Mells to the Mendip limestone. It is nearly

Notes and References

all tarmac now. *See* Intro. to O.S. Map of Neolithic Wessex, 1932, p. 14. The other from Salisbury and Wilton runs over White Sheet Hill as a trackway, passes through a remnant of Selwood at Stourton Tower and becomes the Hardway east of Bruton.

The Roman road ran from Salisbury over Brimsdown Hill north of Maiden Bradley and along the Mendip ridge, perhaps to a fort at Uphill.

23. L. V. Grinsell: Arch. of W., p. 279, J. N. L. Myres: "Wansdyke and the Origins of Wessex" in *Essays in Brit. Hist.*, ed. H. R. Trevor-Roper, 1965, p. 24.

24. A.-S. C. Annal 593.

25. Lady Fox: *South West England*, London, 1964, p. 157.

26. A. L. F. Rivet: *Town and Country in Roman Britain*. London, 1958, p. 153.

27. Lady Fox: *South West England*, p. 144.

28. Another view is that this was the beginning of "the massive Saxon attack on Dumnonia which began in 614". Hoskins: West Exp. of W., p. 4. The position of Bindon between the Axe Estuary and the coast makes it look as though the battle of Beandun was somebody's last stand. Hence the mention of 2,065 Welsh who were killed. See A.-S. C. for 614.

29. A. L. F. Rivet: *Town and Country in Roman Britain*, p. 140. R. G. Collingwood and J. N. L. Myres: *Roman Britain and the English Settlements*. Oxford, 1936, p. 167.

30. Finberg: *Lucerna*, pp. 86–87.

31. Finberg: D. and C., p. 16, No. 72.

32. Lady Fox: *South West England*, p. 117.

33. Ibid., p. 157.

34. R. G. Collingwood and J. N. L. Myres: *Roman Britain and the English Settlements*, p. 316.

35. Lady Fox: *South West England*, p. 169.

36. G. M. Trevelyan: *History of England*. London, 1926, p. 42.

37. A. G. C. Turner: P.S.A.N.H.S., 1951, p. 152. A "saint" in this connotation was simply a clergyman, generally a monk.

38. Lady Fox: *South West England*, pp. 165 and 166.

39. C. A. Ralegh Radford: P.S.A.N.H.S., 1962, pp. 32–35.

40. A.-S. C., Annal 634.

41. Recent drainage schemes have made great improvements, but artificial control of flooding the Somerset "moors" has been an established procedure since at least 1300: "The thick water" of floods is said to be as good as manure. *See* Desmond Hawkins: *Sedgemoor and Avalon*. London, 1954.

42. The mediaeval forest was not all woodland, but an area where deer roamed in the wild state, and the King owned fiercely preserved hunting rights. A "perambulation" of Selwood took place in 1298, but there was not much walking about it. The easier course was taken of making a jury give evidence as to the bounds, starting, but only verbally, at the bridge of Suthbrewham (South Brewham). *See* The Rev. W. H. P. Greswell: *Forests and Deer Parks of the County of Somerset*. Taunton, 1905, p. 266.

43. M. A. W. Sandford: Chapter on "Political History" in V.C.H. Som., Vol. II, 1911.

44. The compiler of the 2nd edition did not consider the evidence from soils adequate.
William of Malmesbury visualised the Glastonbury of A.D. 63 as "a certain island, surrounded by woods, thickets and marshes". Wm. of M: De Ant., p. 2. He had nothing to go by except Glastonbury of the mid-twelfth century.

45. R. H. Hodgkin: Hist. of A.-S., Vol. I, p. 313.
H. P. R. Finberg: *Lucerna*, p. 103 puts forward the same idea, pointing out that such peaceful penetration is bound to lead to "incidents", leading on to the "protection" of its colonists by the stronger power and so to annexation.

46. Hodgkin: Hist. of A.-S., p. 316.

47. Oman: Eng. before N.C., p. 328. Ine's Laws are mentioned later.

48. H. P. R. Finberg in *Lucerna*, p. 93 states that "By 600 the English had begun to settle in mid-Somerset". There appears to be no evidence in support of this date.

49. Freeman: Ine II, p. 16.

50. Wm. of M: De Gestis R., Bk. I, Ch. I, and A.-S C., A.648 and F.648.

51. Bede: E. H., Bk. III, Ch. 7, p. 149.

52. Albany Major: E. W. of W., p. 50.

53. D.N.B., Vol. IX, p. 423.

54. Ethelwerd's "Chronicle", Annal 652. Printed in *Six Old English Chronicles*, ed. J. A. Giles. London, 1896.

55. A.-S. C. translated and ed. D. Whitelock, D. C. Douglas and S. I. Tucker. London, 1961, p. 20 Note.

56. Freeman: Ine I, p. 41.

57. Freeman: Ine II, p. 19 and p. 21.
It later became part of the diocese for Wiltshire and Berkshire with the bishop's see at Ramsbury, a village near Marlborough. Freeman thinks this diocese was carved out of that of Winchester in 909. Carved stones of the early Saxon Church are on view in the present parish church. *See* Ine II, p. 32.
Malmesbury Abbey was founded in the early seventh century by Maildubh from Ireland.

58. It is thought that the parts of the Church walls up as far as the string course are those built for Aldhelm, but that the portions above that level, including the arcading, date from the end of the tenth century.

59. D. P. Dobson-Hinton: *The Archaeology of Somerset*. London, 1931, pp. 207 and 248.

60. There are other theories as to the identity of Penselwood. Albany Major refers to Freeman's doubts expressed in *Old English History* and his suggestion, while not rejecting Penselwood, that Pen Hill on Mendip, two miles N.N.E. of Wells or else Pen or Ben Knoll two miles W. of Wells

might be the place. (The second is a most unlikely spot, and was probably an island in a swamp in 658. It is impossible to imagine any army being chased from Wells over the wet Brent Marsh of those days, over the River Brue and over the Polden Hills to the Parrett). Albany Major also refers to Kerslake's suggestion of Poyntington near Sherborne, but in the end says "On the whole, we see no reason for rejecting the general opinion in favour of Penselwood". *See* E. W. of W., p. 45.

See also the chapter on political history by M. A. W. Sandford in V.C.H. Som. II, p. 176. Kerslake identifies Penn with Poyntington, Earle, Freeman and Ramsey with Penselwood; the latter adds "perhaps one of the Mendips"—whatever in that peakless range a Mendip may be. Ramsey may have been thinking of Pen Hill.

A.-S. C., p. 21, Annal 658. Note 1 says, "Usually identified as Penselwood. Rositzke suggests Pen Pits, Wiltshire; W. G. Hoskins in West Exp. of W. Leicester, 1961, p. 15f either Pinn Beacon (at the south end of East Hill and one and a half miles west of Sidmouth) or Pinhoe, Devon". Pinhoe is three miles N.E. of Exeter.

The Editors of *Place-Names of Devon*, J. E. B. Gover, A. Mawer and Sir Frank Stenton say, p. xvi, that there is no reason to doubt that this battle was fought in the immediate neighbourhood of Penselwood.

Lastly, if there is no evidence that the Saxons entered Somerset in 577, and if they did not enter it at Penselwood, we must confess that we know nothing about the Saxon conquest of Somerset.

61. Wm. of M: De Gestis R., p. 20. The Latin is: "Britannos antiquae libertatis conscientiam frementes et ob hoc crebram rebellionem meditantes, bis omnino protrivit, primum in loco qui dicitur Wirtgernesburg, secundo juxta montem qui dicitur Penne". This might look like a literary touch if the Welsh hatred of the Saxons were not so well known.

62. Flor. of Worc., Annal 657. There is a discrepancy in the date.

63. Hy. of Hunt: Annal 658. "Cenwalh . . . pugnavit contra Brittanos apud Pennum . . . Prima quidem collisione Brittones Anglos aliquantulum repulerunt; cum autem Angli magis horrerent fugam quam mortem, et in repercutiendo persisterent defatigati sunt Brittani, et more nivis liquefacta est vis eorum. Dederunt ergo terga percutientibus, et fugati sunt a Pennum usque ad Pedredan; et facta est super progenium Bruti plaga insanabilis in die illa".

64. Ekwall gives the first recorded form of South Petherton as Sudperet and the Domesday Book version as Sudperetone, the tun on the River Parrett. This is shaky because North Petherton is not on the Parrett at all. Puriton in Domesday is Peritone, pear-tree tun.

65. Ethelwerd: Annal 658.

66. H. E. Winbolt: *Somerset*, London, 1929, p. xxiv. It is difficult to see how this disuse of the Fosse Way can be proved. Grinsell: Arch. of W., p. 258 says that the Fosse Way may have been "a frontier-line even more than a road, though it was certainly both". I. D. Margary in *Roman Roads in Britain*, Vol. I, London, 1955, p. 104 shows that the normal route from London to Exeter was through Dorchester. The Fosse Way ran to Axmouth or Seaton and crossed the two Exeter–Dorchester roads. Otherwise, at its south-western end it ran nowhere that mattered.

67. E. W. and J. H. Wade: *Somerset* (The Little Guides. Methuen and Batsford. London, 10th edition 1949), p. 151.

68. Oman dissents from this, the old view. In Eng. before N.C., p. 286, he says, "The second battle must have been a considerable victory, as we are told that the Britons were driven beyond (sic) the Parret (Pedrida). Yet it does not seem that the borders of Wessex were extended to that limit, the conquest of Mid-Somersetshire being reserved for one of Coenwalch's successors".
   Stenton in A.-S. Eng. (p. 63) and his fellow editors of P.N.D., Vol. I (pp. xvi and xviii) think that probably the battle carried the Saxons as far as the hills between Somerset and Devon. This appears to be unsupported by any documentary or archaeological evidence. As to place names, it would be too much to claim that those of Somerset, few or none of them in writing from the seventh century, are such that the period when they were first used in their original form can be deduced and then used to indicate the time of Saxon settlement within twenty or thirty years. Even written land-charters were not used until Archbishop Theodore (668–90) introduced them. How many of those early ones still exist?

69. Armitage Robinson: *Som. Hist. Essays 1921*, p. 34.
   The Brent Knoll story is very curious. The Glastonbury tradition was that Arthur had himself given Brent Knoll to the Abbey because he blamed himself for the death there of a young man called Yder. Wm. of M: De Ant., p. 70 states that in A.D. 690 King Ine re-granted 10 hides at Brent "which land Abbot Brithwald (had) deserted on his own motion". The Abbot also gave up his office at Glastonbury, but was later made Archbishop of Canterbury.

70. The antiquity of Glastonbury has been an insoluble problem for at least eight centuries. If we can no longer rely on the story of the grant of land by a king of Dyfnaint in 601 (Wm. of M: De Ant., Ch. xxxv and De Gestis R., Bk. I, Ch. I), there is the evidence of the Welsh triad naming "the Three Perpetual Choirs of Britain; the choir of Llan Iltud Vawr in Glamorganshire, the choir of Ambrosius in Ambresbury (Amesbury) and the choir of Glastonbury. In each of these choirs there were 2400 saints, that is, there were a hundred for every hour of the day and night in rotation". Lomax in Wm. of M: De Ant., p. xi gives as reference Probert Triad 84, Guest OC II, 191. See also G. Ashe: *King Arthur's Avalon*, London, 1957, p. 67, for the quotation above.
   As Amesbury fell into the hands of pagan Saxons, and is believed to have been demolished by them, in 554, Glastonbury must have been flourishing before that date—unless the Triad is referring to what has passed, which does not seem to be so.
   Dr. C. A. Ralegh Radford, in relation to recent finds on Glastonbury Tor, said in 1965 that he had been driven to the conclusion that the Abbey did not go back before A.D. 600, or possibly A.D. 550 on its present site—adding that there was no evidence that it was on its present site in the sixth century. (*The Times*, 23rd August, 1965.)
   Mr. G. Ashe considers that "On the whole 385 seems a plausible date for the pioneers". *King Arthur's Avalon*, p. 69.

71. Wm. of M: De Gestis R., p. 22.
   For other psycho-physical effects, see Wm. of M: De Ant., p. 16, "A mysterious odour of Divine sanctity", and for panic terror, pp. 31–32 in Ch. xviii.

72. Mr. Ashe says on p. 169 of *King Arthur's Avalon* that "Cenwalh's treatment of Glastonbury was one of the truly regal gestures of history". It is hard to see why, as the place was too poor to rob and Cenwalh at this stage of his career was a Christian again.

73. G.C. gives the charter as No. 644 (p. 365). "Carta Cenwalh Regis West-saxonie de Manencia de Ferramere DC lxx", and the abbot was Beorth-wald.
    Wm. of M: De Ant, p. 67 "The same king also gave Beokerie (Beckery in Glastonbury), Godenie, Martynesye and Andreyesie", three islands in the marsh.
    See also Finberg: Wessex, p. 109. This charter of Cenwalh's gets two stars from Prof. Finberg, signifying "available in later copy, thought to embody substance of original but having some (possibly spurious) material interpolations".
    For a critical discussion of this charter *see* Armitage Robinson: *Som. Hist. Essays*, 1921, pp. 47–53.

74. G. Ashe: *King Arthur's Avalon*, p. 169 refers to this first belief.
    Wm. of M: De Gestis R., p. 21. "Moreover there are documents of no small credit which have been discovered in certain places, to the following effect: No other hand than those of the disciples of Christ erected the Church of Glastonbury. Nor is it dissonant from probability . . .".

75. Wm. of M: De Ant., p. 34. "So great indeed was his skill in this work that he took from the Church none of its sanctity, while he increased its beauty in many ways."
    Lomax in a note (Wm. of M: De Ant., p. 33) says that Paulinus was a Roman missionary and the Celts would have nothing to do with him. He suggests that he has been confused with Paul Hen i.e. Paul the Aged, preceptor of St. David. Presumably this is the Paulinus who converted Edwin, King of Northumbria. He fled to Kent when Edwin was killed and became bishop of Rochester about 633.

76. For a plan, *see* W. Ashe: *King Arthur's Avalon*, p. 174.

77. Freeman: Ine II, pp. 39, 41 and 42.

78. Armitage Robinson: *Som. Hist. Essays*, p. 35.

79. Saxon monks were introduced into the Abbey by tactful stages. G. Ashe: *King Arthur's Avalon*, p. 171.

80. But it does seem incredible that Centwine, Caedwalla and Ine should all have ended in much the same way.

81. Freeman: Ine II, p. 8, P.N.D., p. xx.

82. Ethelwerd: Annal 682.

83. Flor. of Worc.: Annal 682.

84. Hy of Hunt.: p. 63. Annal 682.

85. Alexander: D.A., LXXII, 1940, p. 106.

86. Hoskins: West Exp. of W., p. 17. "The total disappearance of purely Cornish names in favour of purely English names for about a dozen miles down the Atlantic coast" is mentioned. Elsewhere, however, the place names of north-east Cornwall and of north and north-west Devon are said strongly to resemble those of west Somerset (p. 10 referring to P.N.D.) This is evidence that the northern "prong" of the Saxon advance reached Bude Bay.
    Does this not, however, run counter to Dr. Hoskins's view that the driving of the Britons to the sea was from the Crediton area, won, according to him, as a result of the battle of Posentesbyrig or Posbury in 661? Were not the settlers at Crediton descendants of Saxons from Dorset "with different habits of place-nomenclature" (P.N.D., p. xx, quoted by Dr. Hoskins), who would have planted Dorset type names on the Atlantic coast?

87. Stenton: A.-S. Eng., p. 67. Reference given: Aldhelmi Opera, ed. R.
Ewald (M.G.H.), pp. 14 and 15. J. J. Alexander states that the relevant
passage occurs in a poem written not later than 695. This is printed in
Appendix A.

Aldhelm's contemporary statement buttresses the account given in
A.-S. C. These two authorities must be preferred to Bede's *Ecclesiastical
History* (Bk. IV, Ch. 12, p. 220) which states that "On the death of
Cenwalh . . . his aldermen undertook the government of the realm,
dividing it between them and ruling ten years . . .Cadwalla deposed and
removed these aldermen, and assumed control himself." Bede was only
one year old when Cenwalh died.

H. P. R. Finberg says in *Lucerna*, p. 99. "We are not told who these
enemies were, but there can be little doubt that they were the Britons of
Dumnonia and that the battles were fought in what is now Devon."

88. A.-S. C., Annal 685. Did Caedwalla contend for the kingdom when
Centwine talked of abdicating? Was it the West Saxon kingdom? Caedwalla seemed fond of laying waste Kent.

Wm. of Malmesbury specifically states in De Gestis P., V., p. 352, § 205
(Rolls Series edition) that Centwine designated Caedwalla as his successor,
"morbo et senio gravis, Ceduallam, regii generis juvenum, successorem
decreverat."

89. G.C. 1. Charter 173, 19 Apr., 1168.
    2. Charter 224, 25 Oct., 1303.
    3. Charter 615, 30 Dec., 1303.
    4. Charter 99. No date.
    5. Charter 114. No date . . .? 1191.

90. The charter of grant appears in W. de G. Birch: *Cartularium Saxonicum*,
3 Vols., London, 1855–93, p. 97, where it is No. 62. It is quoted by
G. B. Grundy in *Saxon Charters of Somerset* (Re-printed in one vol.
from P.S.A.N.H.S. in 1935 and published by the Society), pp. 51–52,
and in H. P. R. Finberg: Wessex, p. 110, No. 361.

The grant was made by Centwine to the abbot Hamegils or Hemgisl
and was of 23 hides in the place next to the "well-known wood which is
called Cantucuudu" (Quantock Wood) with 3 hides or cassati south of the
River Tan (Tone)" at the island near the hill called in the British language
Cructan (Barrow by the Tone) but with us Crycbeorh" (Cryc Barrow;
"Cryc" is the Celtic "cruc" and means barrow, anyhow). "And this part
of the land is surrounded by very clearly marked boundaries, for it has
on the south Blacanbroc (Black Brook) and on the north the Tan (Tone)."
The date is 672, believed to be an error for 682.

Wm. of M: De Ant., p. 68, Ch. XXVII mentions the grant under a
sub-heading Munecatone and includes 20 hides in Caric (Cary).

Prof. Finberg says, "The date of the text, 672, lay outside Centwine's
reign, and is contradicted by the indiction (10), which points to 682." He
grades the charter as one "available in a later copy thought to embody
the substance of the original but with some, possibly spurious, material
interpolations".

Another possible shadow of doubt is thrown on this grant of Centwine's
by a charter, of undoubted authenticity in Prof. Finberg's view, by which
Ine granted 20 cassati by the River Tan or Tone to Glastonbury in 705 or
706. It is odd that this estate does not seem to be identifiable unless it was
West Monkton. It might be a confirmation in possession, or it might be

an original grant, but the figures (23 hides on one side of the Tone and 3 on the other against a total of 20) do not tally.

There is also a possibility mentioned later that there has been some confusion over Tan and Tamar in connection with Ine's grant of land, also 20 hides, in 705. This land is believed to have been between the Tamar and the River Lynher.

If it could be proved that it was Ine who first granted land by the Tone at West Monkton and Creech Barrow, the charter of Centwine would have to be treated as a forgery, but there is no need to do that at present.

91. Oman: Eng. before N.C., p. 286.

92. Bede, E.H., Bk. IV, Ch. 12, p. 220.

93. Oman: Eng. before N.C., p. 289.

94. *See* Note 87.

95. Albany Major: E.W. of W., p. 63. He thinks that the Quantocks must have been a "march" or border country until long after the days of Ine, because so many place-names are Saxon references to the Welsh.

96. Albany Major: E. W. of W., pp. 61–62. Of the great Romano–British stronghold he says (p. 60) that St. George Gray proved that, though of pre-Roman origin, it was occupied in Roman and Romano-British times. While it was in British hands, no Saxon advance between the Brendons and the Quantocks was possible.

There would have been no sense in manning the camp with armed Dumnonians in Romano–British times except when a Saxon advance was expected, i.e. between 658 and 682, so it must have been occupied between those dates. But it may have been more of a Dumnonian trade centre than a fort.

> Norton was a market town
> When Taunton was a vuzzy (furzey) down.

(The same rhyme has been used for Crediton and Exeter.)

What is unthinkable is that Ine should have fortified Taunton without having abolished this menace two miles away, or that Centwine should have granted land at West Monkton in 682 without having done so.

For the theory that Ine had his fort here and not where Taunton now is, see later.

97. D.N.B., Vol. IX, p. 422.

98. W. H. P. Greswell: *Dumnonia and the Valley of the Parret*. Taunton, 1922, pp. 110 et seq.

99. Hodgkin: Hist. of A.-S., pp. 315 and 318.

100. Freeman: Ine I, p. 44.

101. V.C.H. Som. I, p. 376.

102. Hoskins: West Exp. of W., p. 19. The date he has in mind is presumably 682 when, he says on p. 18, the Saxons virtually completed their conquest of Devon, a statement we are unable to agree with.

He claims that all the surviving Celtic names are on the Devon side of the county boundary with Somerset.

103. Albany Major: E. W. of W., p. 68.

104. E. T. MacDermot: *The History of the Forest of Exmoor*. Taunton, 1911, p. 2.
P.N.D., p. XX.

105. He says that "-ingtun" names in Haytor and Coleridge Hundreds point to the early sharing out of the best estates among the Saxon leaders, and that a few names like Denbury suggest places where the Britons resisted. Alexander: D.A., LXXII, 1940, p. 106.

106. Hoskins: Devon, p. 43 and West Exp. of W., p. 17.

107. E. T. MacDermot: *Hist. of Forest of Exmoor,* p. 2.

108. P.N.D., p. xx.

109. Ibid.

110. Grinsell: Arch. of W., p. 131.

111. Other figures are 2065 and 2046. Ethelwerd gives "2040 and more".

112. Hoskins: West Exp. of W., pp. 14-16.

113. Alexander: D.A., LXXI, 1939, p. 113.

114. Hodgkin: Hist. of A.-S., pp. 314-316.

115. Alexander: D.A., LXXI, 1939, p. 113.

116. Aileen Fox: *South West England.* London, 1964, p. 157. "Long before the Emperor Honorius wrote to the cities of Britain to tell them that henceforth they must fend for themselves, it is apparent that the mechanism of the Civitas Dumnoniorum was running down."

117. Prof. Hoskins claims that the battle fought at Posentesbyrig in 661 and supposed to have been a Saxon defeat at Pontesbury in Shropshire leading to the harrying of Berkshire by Wulfhere of Mercia (this is not specifically stated to be the consequence, but is mentioned in the same sentence in the A.-S. C.) was in fact a Saxon victory at Posbury outside Crediton. He claims the authority of W. H. Stevenson for this alteration of place. Considering the way in which the battle of Fethanleag has been pushed around the map, one is not surprised, or capable of surprise. The cause of the battle, if in Shropshire, may well have been that Cenwalh was conducting a flank attack on the Mercians who were always trying to "adjust" his northern frontier. Oman: Eng. before N.C., p. 287 suggests that Cenwalh "must have been advancing in company with Eanfrith, King of the Hwiccas, to execute a diversion in favour of their ally and suzerain, Oswy".

No one has previously mentioned Postlebury, the name of a hill, farm and wood on the edge of Selwood Forest, a likely site for a return match after the battle of Penselwood 6 miles away and only three years before. Postlebury is four miles south-west of Frome.

118. Freeman says that the only written support for this is in some documents of Bishop Grandison in the fourteenth century. (Ine II, p. 6.)

W. H. Stevenson claimed that the great number of Saxon names in the great charter of 739 proved that there was a considerable English settlement in the Crediton neighbourhood some time before the date of the charter. Prof. Hoskins refers to "The Crawford Collection of Early Charters", ed. by A. S. Napier and W. H. Stevenson in *Anecdota Oxoniensia,* Oxford, 1895, p. 44. *See* Hoskins: West Exp. of W., p. 14.

The Editors of P.N.D., p. xv, say they cannot trust these names as original—and they would not necessarily go back to 680—while Prof. D. Whitelock says that this charter of 739 has "some suspicious features in a hand of the mid-eleventh century". E.H.D. I, p. 455.

119. Hoskins: Devon, p. 221.

120. Hoskins: West Exp. of W., p. 17.

Notes and References

121. Finberg: *Lucerna*, p. 102.

122. Alexander: D.A., LXXII, 1940, p. 106.

123. Wm. of M: De Gestis R., p. 31.

124. The lignea basilica or wooden church is specifically mentioned as the place of signature in the charter of 704 by which Ine exempted Glastonbury Abbey from "all troubles of taxation". "Actum et confirmatum in lignea basilica anno ab incarnacione Domini DCC iiij." If the charter was a forgery, this was a fine piece of local colour and corroborative evidence. *See* G.C., p. 141, Charter 200.

125. Wm. of M: De Ant., p. 73. Mul was the brother of Caedwalla, Ine's predecessor. It has been suggested that Mul and Ine were sons of a Welsh woman i.e. half-brothers. Hence Ine's civilised treatment of the Welsh in his Laws. *See* article by W. Hunt in D.N.B., Vol. XXVIII, 1891, pp. 428–430.
    The wergild paid by the Kentish people for burning Mul alive was 30,000 pieces of money: Ethelwerd and Florence of Worcester say 30,000 gold solidi, equal to 3,750 pounds of gold in weight. Oman: Eng. before N.C., p. 327. A.-S. C., ed. Garmonsway, p. 40, Note 1.

126. Wm. of M: De Ant., p. 75.

127. G.C., pp. 450, 495 and 527, but the charter on p. 527 gives a date, 663, before Ine was king.

128. Wm. of M: De Ant., p. 72; A. of D., pp. 52, 96, 97.

129. A.-S. C., Annal 715. The alternative site is Wanborough just south-east of Swindon, close to a Roman road where it crosses the Ridgeway. Ceawlin and Ine seem to have fought hard battles at the same spot, but with different types of enemy and different results.

130. A.-S. C., Annals 721, 722 and 725.
     W. Hunt in D.N.B., Vol. XXVIII, pp. 428–430.

131. E.H.D. I, pp. 364–372.

132. Centwine's grant of West Monkton and Creech Barrow included 3 hides south of the Tone.

133. For instance, E. A. Freeman: Ine I, p. 43, where he says that the River Tone may have been the frontier from 682 to 710, and E. T. MacDermot: *Hist. of Forest of Exmoor*, p. 1.

134. Alexander: D.A., LXXI, 1939, p. 113.

135. A. W. Vivian Neal and H. St. G. Gray: "Materials for the History of Taunton Castle", P.S.A.N.H.S., LXXXVI, 1940.
     C. A. Ralegh Radford and A. D. Hallam: "The History of Taunton Castle in the Light of Recent Excavations". P.S.A.N.H.S., XCVIII, 1953, pub. 1955.

136. Oman: Eng. before N.C., p. 37. He called himself in legal documents "Ego Nodelmus rex Suthsaxonum". Was Noon's Barrow named after him and, if so, why?

137. Bede: E.H., p. 299.

138. Finberg: D. and C., p. 16, quoting BM Cotton MS Faust Aii, fo 246.

139. Finberg: *Lucerna*, p. 88.

140. Flor. of Worc., Annal 710.

141. Hy of Hunt., Annal 710, p. 111.
142. Alexander: D.A. LXXII, 1940, p. 106 and D.A. LXXIII, 1941, p. 95.
143. *Annales Cambriae*, ed. Rev. J. W. ab Ithel, London, 1860, p. 15. The entry shows that three centuries after Dyrham, the Welsh of Wales looked on the King of Cornwall as one of their own people still.
144. D.N.B., Vol. XXVIII, p. 429. Article on Centwine by The Rev. Wm. Hunt. It is interesting to observe that Ethelwerd does say under 721, "After seven years Ina slew Cynewulf, and after six months made war against the Southern English". The date previous to 721 is 715, but it is not the rebellion that is recorded then.
145. Flor. of Worc., Annals 722 and 725.
     Hy of Hunt., p. 112, Annal 725.
146. Freeman: Ine I, p. 50.
147. Oman: Eng. before N.C., p. 329.
     There are some, including Oman, who give the date of these battles as 721. In fact, they appear under CCLXXVIII Annus, which J. W. ab Ithel, editor of *Annales Cambriae* in the Rolls Series, Longmans, 1860, equates with the year 722 of the Christian era. The first annus to the compiler of *Annales Cambriae* was A.D. 444.
     Even if the Saxon defeat at Hehil was in 721, and not while Ealdberht was making a nuisance of himself at Taunton in 722, Ine's absence from Taunton is still accounted for. In the circumstances, he would have had urgent matters to deal with on his Devon frontier.
148. *Annales Cambriae*, as above. Annal 722.
149. Oman: Eng. before N.C., p. 329, Note 1.
150. D.N.B., Vol. XXVIII, 1896, p. 429. Article by Rev. Wm. Hunt on Ine. Hunt is not referring specifically to 722.
151. Alexander: D.A., LXXIII, 1941, p. 95. *See also* Hoskins: West Exp. of W., p. 18.
152. Alexander: D.A., 1940, p. 106.
153. G.C., pp. cxcviii and 580, Ch. 1066 c. 1245.
     The Priory of Lamana appears on p. 78 Charter 126 (an agreement between Glastonbury and the Bishop of Wells—with, in the margin, "Nota de quadam cella in Cornubia vocata Lamana") and in a judgement of the Pope, allowing the monks and not the Bishop to have Lamana (p. xliii). On p. 128 in Charter 173 Pope Alexander III confirms the monks' tenure of certain properties, including Lamana. There are also references to the payment of feudal dues related to Lamana, pp. 580 and cxcvii, Ch. 1066, 1245 and to the remission of a tenant's service of transporting monks to Cornwall, p. 445, Ch. 810, May, 1264.
     For ruins of buildings, *see* Pevsner: *Buildings of England: Cornwall*, Penguin Books, p. 92. *Little Guide to Cornwall*, 9th edition, 1950, p. 107 and Arthur Mee's *Cornwall*, p. 127.
154. Adam of Domerham: *Historia de Rebus Glastoniensibus* includes the classic printed version of William of Malmesbury's *De Antiquitate*, taken from the MS owned by Trinity College, Cambridge. T. Hearne edited it and it was published at Oxford in 1727. This states, p. 48, that "Anno Dominicae Incarnacionis Sexcentesimo primo rex Domnoniae terram, quae appellatur Yneswitrin, ad Ecclesiam vetustam concessit, quae ibi sita est, ob peticionem Worgret abbatis, in quinque cassatis". The document claims to have been written by Mauuron, a bishop with a

distinctly Welsh-sounding name, and Worgret, the petitioning abbot, subscribed it. "Who this king was the age of the document prevents one from knowing". William ends up with a sneer at Worgret's name, "which smacks of British barbarism".

This is all more than mysterious, for Prof. H. P. R. Finberg has pointed out that scholars are now generally agreed that written land-grants came in with Archbishop Theodore about 668 and that no charter could have been dated as 601, as the Incarnation was not used as a chronological basis until the middle of the seventh century. He thinks that the grant of Yneswitrin may have been ante-dated by at least three-quarters of a century and that the date is probably about 700. *See* his *Lucerna*, pp. 86 and 87.

Could William have mis-read DCCI as DCI? (In William's book the year is not in Roman numerals but in words. "Anno Dominicae Incarnacionis sexcentesimo primo"). Unfortunately, that will not fit in with the British name of Worgret and the names of his successors Lademund and Bregored, for Charter 818 shows Ine giving land at Doulting in 702 to Abbot Beorwaldo. Charter 774, which is probably the correct version, shows the same grant in 705. William of Malmesbury: *De Antiquitate*, Ch. XXXVIII, p. 72, says Berwald succeeded in the year 705 (and was given 20 hides close to "Tamar" by Ine). Prof. Finberg says he can find no independent evidence that the Britons called Glastonbury Yneswitrin —but this word is the sole link with Ine as a possible giver-away of land in Cornwall, Linig having disappeared from the map.

See Adam of Domerham, p. 96 also. The English after conversion gave back Brent and Polden "cum pluribus aliis unde rex Domnoniae dedit terram, appellatum Yneswitherim V hidas".

155. Wm. of M: De Ant., p. 72.

156. A. of D., pp. 52 (and Note 1—Linis, supra lin, et alia manu) and 97.

157. A. of D. says that Ine gave Glastonbury 20 hides at Brent Marsh, 12 at Sowy, 20 at Pilton, 20 at Doulting, 20 next to Tamer, namely Linig, and 20 hides at Rouelt and elsewhere one hide with fishing rights. A note says that Famer has been written for Tamer in another copy (p. 97). The same book elsewhere, after the Privilegium Ine, records a grant to Berwald in 705 of 20 hides, "juxta Tamer", 20 hides in Bouelt, 12 in Sowy (Zoy) 5 in Corregs (Croscombe), half a hide with fishing rights in Escford, and 20 hides in Doulting. After the statement "Ego Aldemus hanc scedulam scripsi" there is added as an afterthought "Dedit (etiam) Ina rex Piltone XX hidas eidem abbati". In another hand "Linis" has been written above the line after Tamer. A. of D., p. 52.

The scribe was not aware, apparently, that the grant of land on both sides of the Doulting stream was a grant of Pilton. *See* note by Dom Aelred Watkin, who points out that the boundaries are identical, in G.C., II clv. (*See* also p. 450, Charter 818.)

John of Glastonbury says the same things on p. 93 of his *Glastoniensis Chronica*, ed. T. Hearne, Oxford, 1726, pp. 41 and 93, but he does not mention Linig here. On p. 41 he does, in a list starting with 20 hides at Brent Marsh.

There are various odd circumstances. Charter 903, dated 725 is a grant of land at Sowy by Ina (G.C., p. 495). Brent Marsh is granted by Ine in Charter 979, dated 20th July 663 long before Ine was King (G.C. p. 527) but 10 hides only. Birch has tentatively corrected the date to 693 or 708. *See* Grundy: *Saxon Charters of Somerset*, p. 149. Grundy says that the

Brent Marsh survey is of "that very earliest type which gives only one landmark for each side of the grant". Brent was said to have been originally granted by Arthur. A. of D., p. 96.

It looks as though some of these charters are omnibus or umbrella affairs "composed" to cover properties, of which the authentic charters of grant had been lost—or had gone up in smoke in the great fire of 1184. They are mostly "pious frauds" and hardly one is what it purports to be.

158. Prof. Hoskins suggests that Linig is derived from the Welsh root Lei, to flow, and the English Ieg, an island or peninsula. Hoskins and Finberg: D.S., p. 60. *See* Finberg: *Lucerna*, p. 90.

159. Finberg: D. and C., p. 16, No. 72.

160. Ibid., p. 16, No. 74.

161. Hoskins and Finberg: D.S., p. 20.

162. G.C., Charter 655, p. 375 and Charter 961, p. 517.

163. Walter de Gray Birch: *Cartularium Saxonicum*. London, 1885, p. 166, No. 113.

164. Finberg: Wessex, p. 112.

165. Finberg: D. and C., p. 7, No. 729.

166. The A.-S. C. entry for 661 reads as though a victorious Mercian king was able after the battle to walk through Wessex doing what he liked. "In this year Cenwealh fought at Easter at Posentesbyrig; and Wulfhere, the son of Penda, harried on (or from) Ashdown. . . . And Wulfhere, the son of Penda, harried in the Isle of Wight, and gave the people of the Isle of Wight to Aethelwold, King of the South Saxons, because Wulfhere had stood sponsor to him at baptism."

This does not look like the consequence of a victory outside Shrewsbury for the West Saxons; neither is it, alternatively, the sort of thing the West Saxons would have allowed to happen if they had been able to win a victory over the West Welsh in mid-Devon, at Posbury outside Crediton, at Easter, the beginning of the campaigning season.

167. If the north-eastern tip of Cornwall—the Hele Bridge–Poundstock area—was being invaded by Ine in 722, it is unlikely to have been conquered in a drive to the sea from central Devon in 682, as Prof. Hoskins would have us believe.

Prof. Hoskins quotes William of Malmesbury as saying that it was Athelstan who fixed the left bank of the Tamar as the county boundary. This was about 926. Hoskins and Finberg: D.S., p. 26.

Appendix A

ST. ALDHELM ON CENTWINE AND HIS THREE BATTLES

From "Aldhelmi Opera". Ed. R. Ehwald. Berlin, 1919, in the series *Monumenta Germaniae Historica*.

p. 14. Part of "Carmina Ecclesiastica III" (In *Ecclesia Mariae A Bugge Exstructa*)

circa 690	Hoc templum Bugge pulchro molimine structum
	Nobilis erexit Centvvini filia regis
676–685	Qui prius imperium Saxonum rite regebat,
	Donec praesentes contemnens culmina regni
	Divitias mundi rerumque reliquit habenas,
	Plurima basilicis impendens rura novellis,
	Qua nunc Christicolae servant monastica iura
p. 15	Exin sacratam perrexit quaerere vitam,
	Dum proprium linquit Christi pro nomine regnum,
10	Qui tamen ante tribus gessit certamina pugnis
	Et ternis pariter confecit bella triumphis.
	Sic rexit regnum plures feliciter annos,
	Donec conversus cellam migravit in almam
	Inde petit superas meritis splendentibus arces
15	Angelicis turmis ad caeli culmina ductus;
	Caelicolis iunctus laetatur sorte superna.

The poem goes on to deal with Caedwalla, introduced thus:

Post hunc successit bello famosus et armis
Rex Caedvvalla, potens regni possessor et heres;

F

73

Appendix B

ARCHAEOLOGICAL EVIDENCE

Reginald A. Smith writes, in the first of the Somerset volumes of the *Victoria County History* (p. 373) in 1906, "The soil of Somerset has yielded next to nothing characteristic of the pagan Saxon". The position in 1966, after many extensive excavations, is practically the same. This tends to prove that the Saxons did not enter Somerset until they were Christians, nominally, at least.

General considerations:

1. It was not until 634 that Birinus started to convert the West Saxons to Christianity: even so, men did not suddenly abandon all their burial customs. "Pagan methods of burial," says Mr. L. V. Grinsell, "continued well into the Christian period" (Arch. of W., p. 294), and Mr. C. W. Phillips in his brilliant introduction to the O.S. Map of Britain in the Dark Ages (2nd edition, 1966, p. 21) says that "It is not till the early 8th century that the older practice dies away".

2. The latter writer also says that "the pagan burials still do not encroach beyond the western limits of Salisbury Plain" (p. 22) and he believes that "On the outer limits of the Anglo-Saxon world in the early 7th century we are entitled to wonder if the possession of no more than a spear and a knife must always be the mark of an Anglo-Saxon burial".

   One could be buried with a Saxon knife or other object at any time after it was made, but one would not have been so buried after the pagan custom of burying weapons and personal ornaments had been abandoned: this happened, not at the period of the Conversion, apparently, but up to almost a century afterwards. Can an iron knife which has been rusting in the ground for centuries be dated?

Buckland Dinham burial. In 1925 Abbot Horne found two skeletons in one grave, with a few other human bones, in a small quarry on Barrow Hill, Buckland Dinham. One skeleton was that of a woman. In the grave

75

were two rings of silver wire and six beads. The burial is said to be a pagan one of the sixth century. (P.S.A.N.H.S., LXXIV, p. lviii, 1928.)

This grave is something of a problem. Although the quarry was worked a little, no other remains were found. The theory of Dr. Myres mentioned below would account for the presence of the grave—but one swallow does not make a summer. Less than a mile away is the road representing the prehistoric trackway from Salisbury Plain to the Mendips (Intro. to O.S. map of Neolithic Wessex, 1932) and the western border of Selwood cannot have been more than five miles to the east.

Camerton Saxon Cemetery. The plateau between Camerton and Radstock, thanks to the lifelong efforts of Mr. W. J. Wedlake, F.S.A., has a well-recorded history from Neolithic to Saxon times. There appears to have been a break in occupation between the abandonment of the Romano-British village by the Fosse Way early in the fifth century and the Saxon occupation, but this interval is not certain.

The Saxon cemetery was discovered by Fr. (later Abbot) Ethelbert Horne when quarrying was going on in 1926, and the site was excavated during the next six years under his direction, with Mr. Wedlake acting as foreman. 109 graves were found, with 115 skeletons, none showing signs of violent death so far as could be ascertained, though one man's foot had been removed, possibly as a punishment for theft, it has been suggested. Some burials are thought to have been those of victims of plague. The lower jaws were well enough preserved to yield accurate measurements and these coincided almost exactly with a series of 66 Anglo-Saxon skull contours measured by Dr. Parsons. The graves were mainly from east to west. Finds included a number of beads, some thought to be of the fifth or the early sixth century. There were 28 iron knives such as have frequently been found in Saxon graves. The most striking objects were two small gilt discs or bracteates, each with a cross, "pattée convexed" as its only ornamentation.

One very notable fact is that small grains of charcoal had been thrown on the bodies at the time of burial in 42 out of 109 graves. Charcoal was never found below the skeleton. In most cases an infant would be buried without charcoal, but it was used for young children. This feature, when Abbot Horne wrote, had not been noticed in any other Saxon cemetery.

The excavations are recorded in articles by Abbot Horne in P.S.A.N.H.S., LXXIV, 1928, and LXXIX, 1933.

Abbot Horne said in his first article, p. 63, that he thought this was a Christian cemetery, and Mr. Wedlake in his *"Excavations at Camerton, Somerset"* (published in 1958 by what is now the Bath and Camerton Archaeological Society) says on p. 96, "The cemetery, judging from the orientation of the graves and the cross on two of the gilt bracteates found, was probably a Christian one . . . it appears to have been in use during the sixth and seventh centuries A.D." It may have been used by Saxon Christians still using pagan burial rites, but it could not have been both Christian and West Saxon before Birinus inaugurated his mission in 634.

Mr. L. V. Grinsell (Arch. of W., p. 280) says that this cemetery was "somewhat in the pagan tradition" and "must have been started after A.D. 658" (battle of Penselwood), but that rather begs the question, Must it?

Mr. C. W. Phillips in his introduction to the new Dark Ages map (p. 26) says that this cemetery, "while clearly Christian, has nothing in it to give it a decisively Saxon character" and he has classified it as Sub-Roman. Could it possibly have been Romano-British Celtic Christian of any part of the fifth century? Six Roman coins were distributed in five graves, but that proves little. (Abbot Horne, P.S.A.N.H.S., LXXIX, 1933, p. 44). Dr. Ralegh Radford holds that the Celtic inhabitants of Somerset were Christians when the Saxons arrived. (Pres. Address, P.S.A.N.H.S., 106, 1962).

Mrs. Audrey Meaney in her *Gazetteer of Early Anglo-Saxon Burial Sites* (London, 1964, p. 218) simply says that the cemetery is of the seventh century.

Sir Cyril and Lady Fox base their theory that West Wansdyke was built by Saxons between 628 and 634 partly on the belief that "By the early seventh century there was Saxon occupation in the area, as the inhumation cemetery of late type at Camerton on the Fossway shows". (*Archaeological Journal*, Vol. CXV for 1958, published 1960.)

Lastly, Dr. J. N. L. Myres, in an article published in 1965 partly to disrupt this argument and cause further consideration of it, throws out the suggestion that some West Saxons could have entered Somerset from Wiltshire through Selwood and that Ceawlin might have built West Wansdyke before 577 to protect his subjects at Camerton and round about from the Britons of Bath, carrying this movement forward later by capturing Bath and winning the battle of Dyrham. (J. N. L. Myres: "Wansdyke and the Origins of Wessex" in *Essays in British History*, ed. H. R. Trevor-Roper, Macmillan, London, 1965.)

Altogether, the Camerton Cemetery seems to provide no satisfactory evidence that Ceawlin's West Saxons entered north Somerset after the battle of Dyrham in 577, nor, of course, does it yield proof that they did not do so.

Cannington Park Quarry Cemetery. This is close to Combwich on the Parrett. In 1907 Albany Major and others made some excavations and thought that almost all the graves, out of a probable thousand, had been quarried away. He connected the cemetery with the defeat of Hubba the Dane by Odda and the West Saxons in 878. Mrs. Dobson-Hinton mentions this as a possibility and points out that in 845 the men of Somerset and Dorset made a great slaughter of the Danes at the mouth of the Parrett. The theory that Cynuit, Hubba's landing-place, was Countisbury seems to be going out of fashion. Combwich would have been a much more sensible place, if it was intended to attack Alfred from the rear. (Albany Major: E. W. of W., pp. 181–193 and D. P. Dobson: *Arch. of Som.*, p. 169).

In 1962/3 Mr. P. A. Rahtz excavated about 300 graves out of an estimated 5000. He found skeletons of men, women and children, all properly laid out, and none with the signs of violent death mentioned by earlier writers. Could there not have been both a civilian and a warrior (i.e. post-battle) cemetery side by side? The inhabitants of the "small and feeble camp of normal plan", as Allcroft calls it, must have buried their dead somewhere.

Mr. C. W. Phillips (Intro. to O.S. Dark Ages map, 2nd edn., p. 26) states that the cemetery was in use from the fourth to possibly the eighth century. Mr. L. V. Grinsell tentatively supports this view (P.S.A.N.H.S., CIX, 1965, p. 64). Inhumations at Banwell and Yatton are regarded as broadly of the same period.

Inhumations have been found at Evercreech (a human skeleton with an Anglo-Saxon knife), at Queen Camel (9 skeletons with an Anglo-Saxon sword), at Saltford (6 graves with an Anglo-Saxon iron knife) and at Upton, Long Sutton, where quarrymen casually and vaguely mentioned extended burials with pottery, coins and buckles. All these are related simply to the Anglo-Saxon period and are useless for our purpose. At Huish Episcopi, however, Mrs. Audrey Meaney reports the remains of three human skeletons, one with a small bronze ring "probably late Roman or of the pagan Anglo-Saxon period, perhaps of the sixth or the seventh century".

Of odd finds, the chief are two disc brooches of the sixth century and of a type common in a Saxon cemetery at Long Wittenham, Berks.; these were found at Ilchester along with a Jutish pattern brooch probably of the second half of the seventh century (Dobson: *Arch. of Som.*, p. 183). These three brooches may well have been handed down from generation to generation before being lost in the ground. (It seems unlikely, but one wonders whether Ilchester, as one of the two cantonal capitals of the Durotriges, fell into the hands of the Saxon victors of Beandun soon after 614: probably not, for it is a fair distance ahead of Penselwood). At Kewstoke a Saxon knife was found in St. Kew's cell and at Ham Hill a reputed Saxon shield boss was discovered. At Worlebury hut circles, a dagger and a spear butt said to be Saxon were found. These rusty objects are useless when we are looking for approximate dating. It would be even more useless to mention objects known to be of the late Saxon period.

If it is clear that in Somerset archaeology at present can throw no light on the Saxon conquest, in Devon things are even worse. In 1906 Mr. R. A. Smith's chapter on "Anglo-Saxon remains" was published in the V.C.H. and he could mention as a relic of the Saxons at the start of the eighth century only one bronze sword guard, engraved "Leofric me fecit".

Index of Persons

mentioned in the text

Index of Persons

Seaxburgh, Queen (Regnant) of the West Saxons, widow of Cenwalh, 28, 31
Sidwell, St., 36
Smith, R. A., 32, 75, 79
Stenton, Sir Frank, 13
Sumorsaetan, The, 32

Trevelyan, G. M., 10, 17
Trevor-Roper, H. R., 77
Turner, A. G. C., 18

Wedlake, W. J., 12, 76
William of Malmesbury, monk and chronicler, 16, 21, 23, 24, 26, 30, 39, 43, 48, 49, 50
Willibald, 36, 37
Winfrith, see St. Boniface
Worcester, Florence of, see Florence of Worcester
Wulfhard or Wulfheard, Abbot at Exeter, 36
Wulfhere, King of the Mercians, 22, 46

Index of Places

mentioned in the text

(Reference to counties have been omitted)